EASY
GUITAR
WITH NOTES & TAB

TAYLOR SWIFT

19

C000203412

ISBN 978-1-4950-0753-8

HAL•LEONARD®
CORPORATION
7777 W. BLUEMOUND RD. P.O. BOX 13819 MILWAUKEE, WI 53213

Visit Hal Leonard Online at
www.halleonard.com

STRUM AND PICK PATTERNS

This chart contains the suggested strum and pick patterns that are referred to by number at the beginning of each song in this book. The symbols ⊓ and ∨ in the strum patterns refer to down and up strokes, respectively. The letters in the pick patterns indicate which right-hand fingers play which strings.

p = **thumb**
i **=** **index finger**
m = **middle finger**
a = **ring finger**

For example; Pick Pattern 2
is played: thumb - index - middle - ring

Strum Patterns   ## Pick Patterns

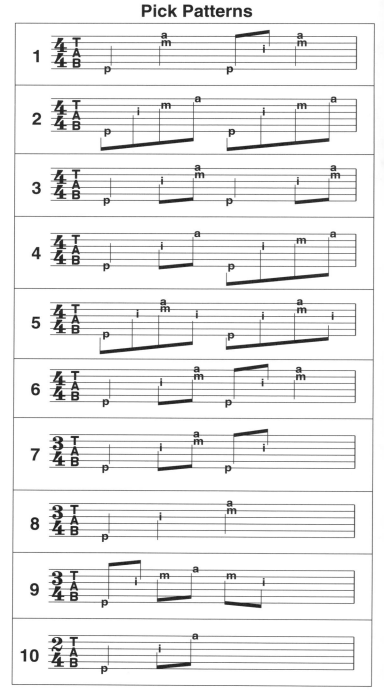

You can use the 3/4 Strum and Pick Patterns in songs written in compound meter (6/8, 9/8, 12/8, etc.). For example, you can accompany a song in 6/8 by playing the 3/4 pattern twice in each measure. The 4/4 Strum and Pick Patterns can be used for songs written in cut time (¢) by doubling the note time values in the patterns. Each pattern would therefore last two measures in cut time.

Welcome to New York

Words and Music by Taylor Swift and Ryan Tedder

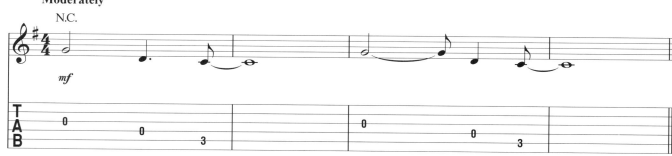

Strum Pattern: 1
Pick Pattern: 5

Intro
Moderately

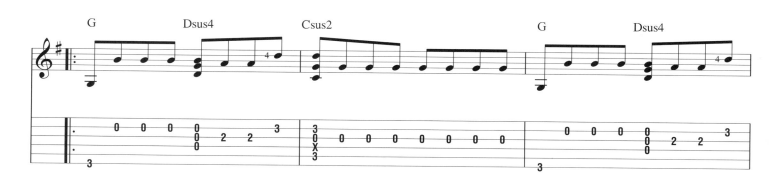

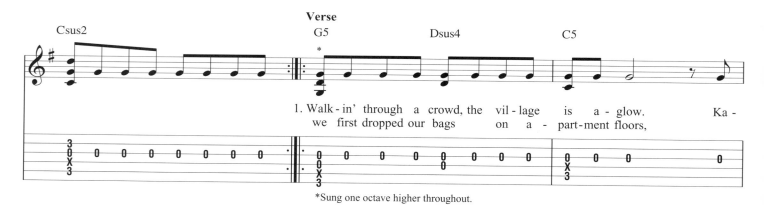

*Sung one octave higher throughout.

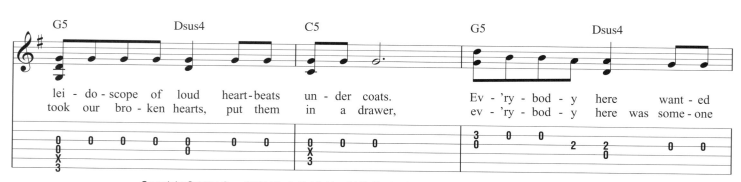

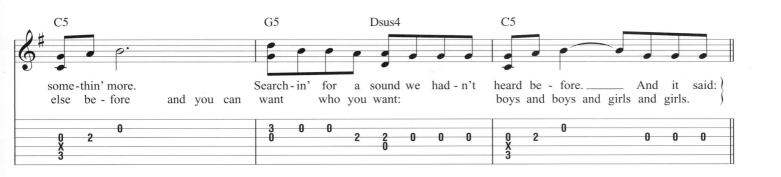

3rd time, To Coda

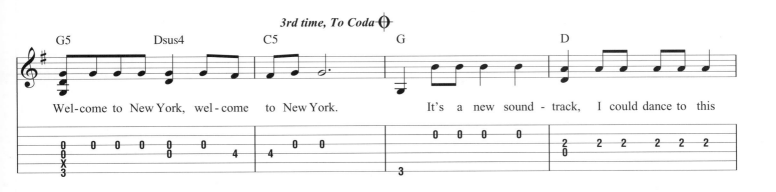

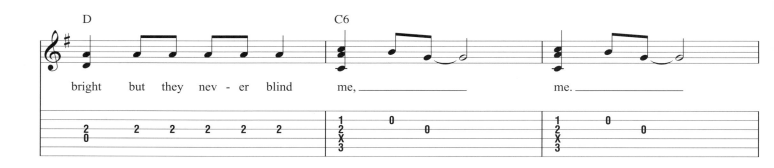

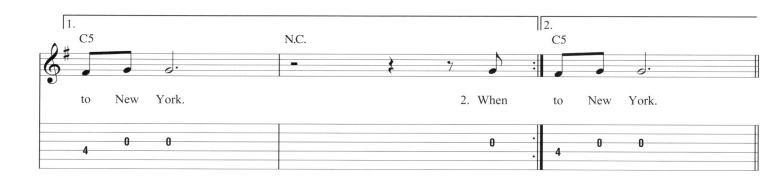

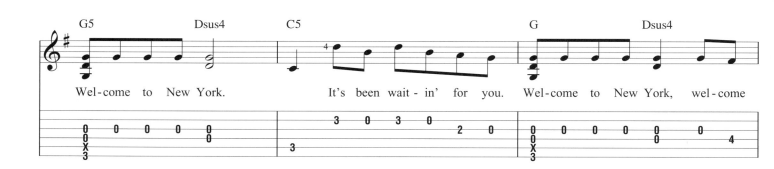

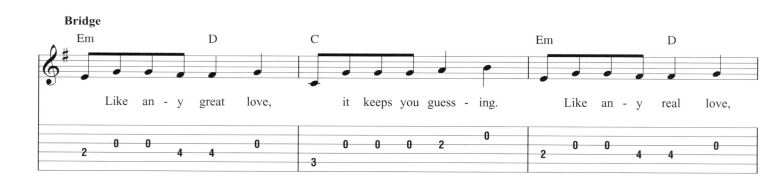

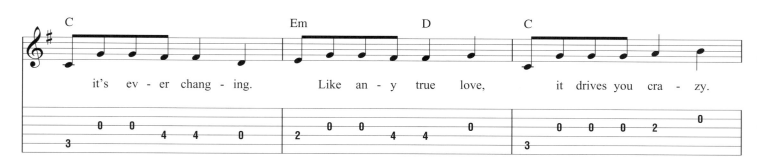

Blank Space

Words and Music by Taylor Swift, Max Martin and Shellback

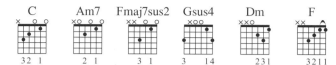

*Capo V

Strum Pattern: 6
Pick Pattern: 4

Intro
Moderately slow

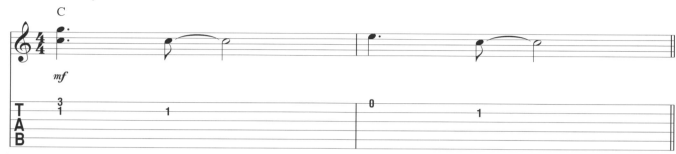

*Optional: To match recording, place capo at 5th fret.

Verse

1. Nice to meet you, where you been? I could show you in-cred-i-ble
2. Cher-ry lips, where crys-tal skies, I could show you in-cred-i-ble

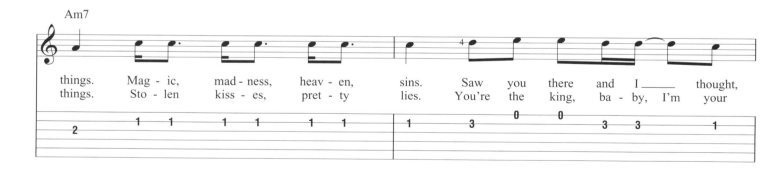

things. Mag-ic, mad-ness, heav-en, sins. Saw you there and I _____ thought,
things. Sto-len kiss-es, pret-ty lies. You're the king, ba-by, I'm your

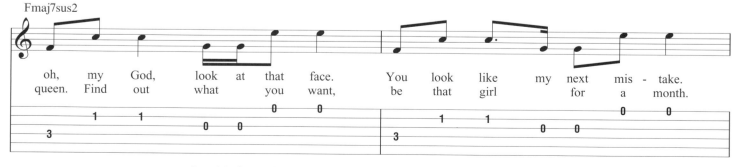

oh, my God, look at that face. You look like my next mis-take.
queen. Find out what you want, be that girl for a month.

Gsus4

Love's a game, wan-na play? _____ Oh, no.
Wait, the worst is yet to come. _____

C

New mon-ey, suit and tie, I can read you like a mag-a-
Scream-ing, cry-ing, per-fect storms. I can make all the ta-bles

Am7

zine. Ain't it fun-ny? Ru-mors fly, and I know you heard a-bout
turn. Rose gar-den filled with thorns. Keep you sec-ond guess-ing like,

Fmaj7sus2

me. So, hey, let's be friends. I'm dy-in' to see how this one ends.
"Oh, my God, who is she?" I get drunk on jeal-ous-y. But

Gsus4   N.C.

Grab your pass - port and my hand. *Spoken: I can make the bad guys good for a weekend.*
you'll come back each time you leave. *'Cause darling, I'm a nightmare dressed like a daydream.*

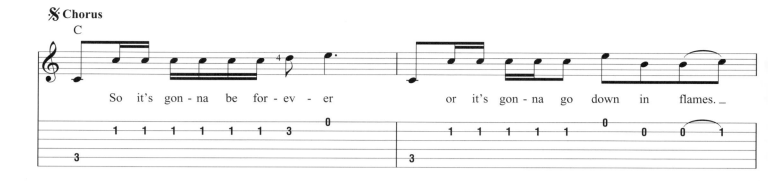

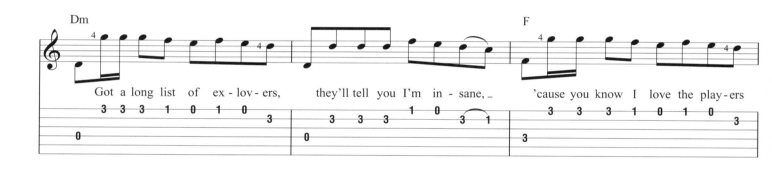

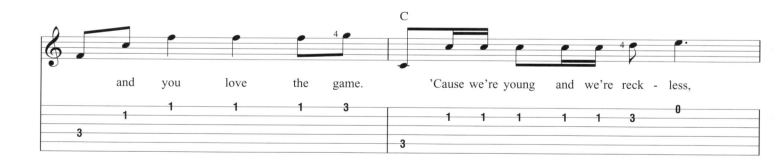

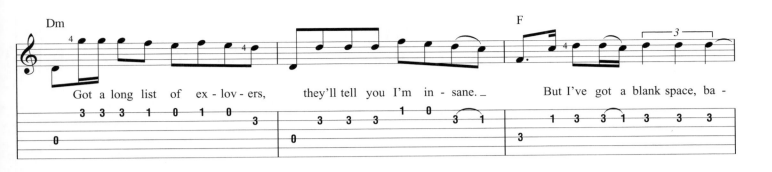

Got a long list of ex - lov - ers, they'll tell you I'm in - sane. __ But I've got a blank space, ba -

3rd time, To Coda ⊕ | 1.

Interlude

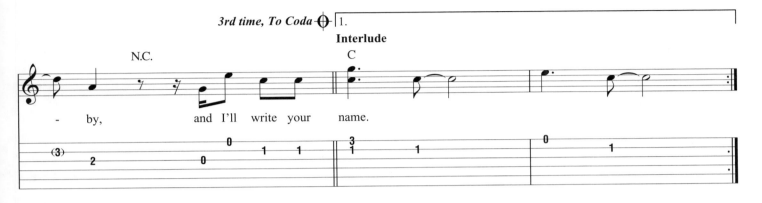

- by, and I'll write your name.

2.

Bridge

name. Boys on - ly want love if it's tor - ture. Don't say I did - n't,

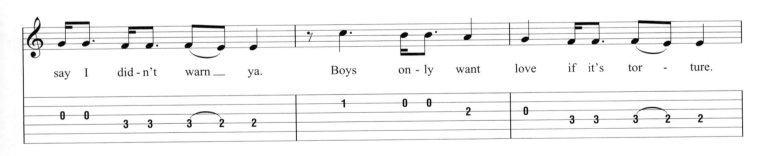

say I did - n't warn __ ya. Boys on - ly want love if it's tor - ture.

D.S. al Coda ⊕ **Coda**

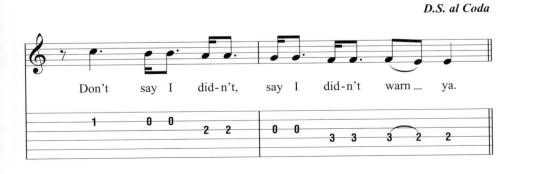

Don't say I did - n't, say I did - n't warn __ ya.

name.

Style

Words and Music by Taylor Swift, Max Martin, Shellback and Ali Payami

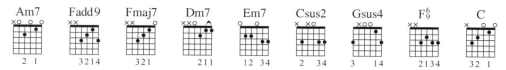

*Capo II

Strum Pattern: 1
Pick Pattern: 5

Intro
Moderately slow, in 2

*Optional: To match recording, place capo at 2nd fret.
**Chord symbols reflect overall harmony.

1. Mid - night, ___ you come and pick ___ me up, no
2. So it goes. ___ He can't keep ___ his wild eyes

head - lights. ___
on the road. ___ Mm. ___

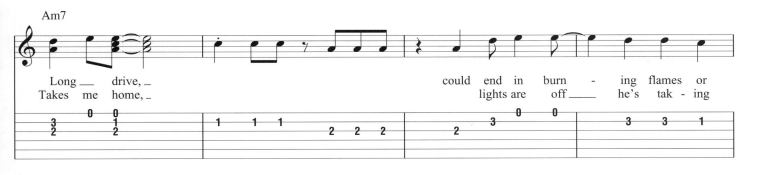

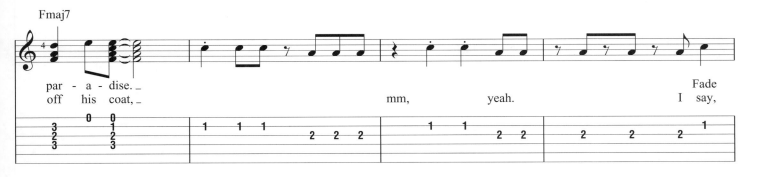

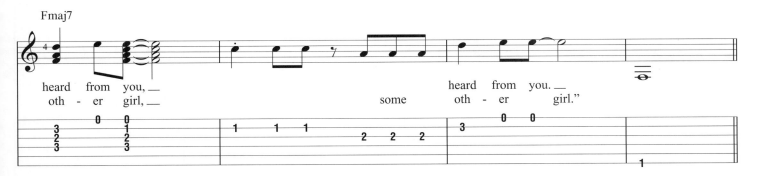

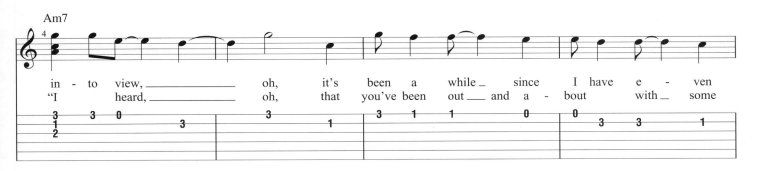

Pre-Chorus

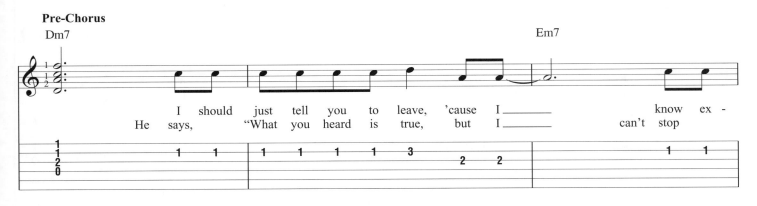

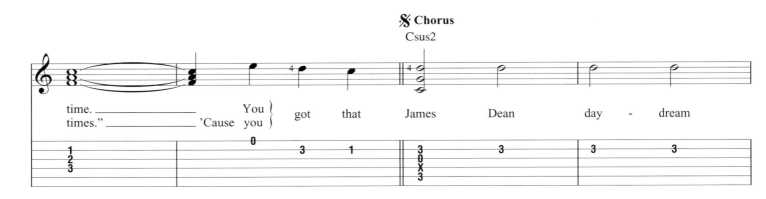

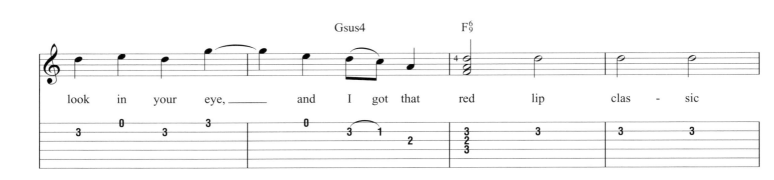

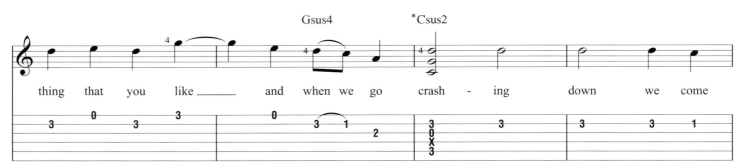

*3rd time, substitute Am7.

3rd time, To Coda ⊕

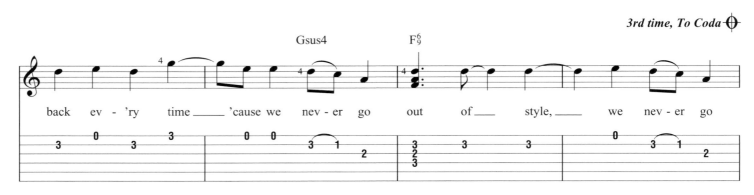

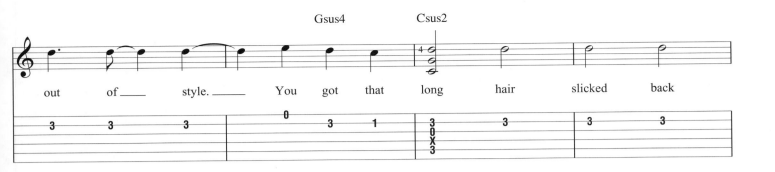

out of ___ style. ___ You got that long hair slicked back

white t - shirt ___ and I got that good girl faith and a

tight lit - tle skirt ___ and when we go crash - ing down we come

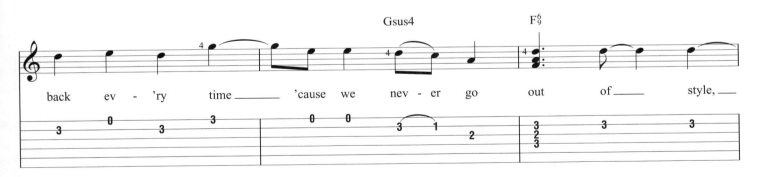

back ev - 'ry time ___ 'cause we nev - er go out of ___ style, ___

___ we nev - er go out of ___ style. ___ ___ Take me home. ___

*Sung one octave higher.

Bridge

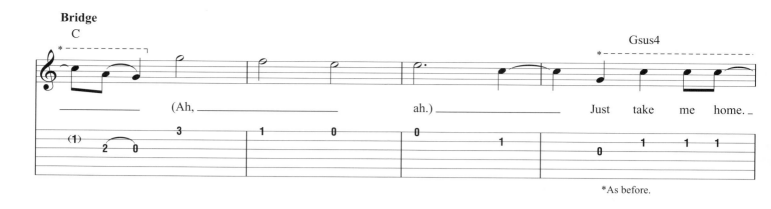

*As before.

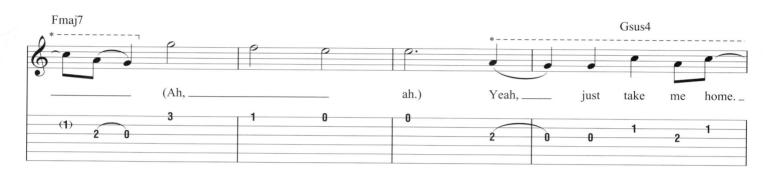

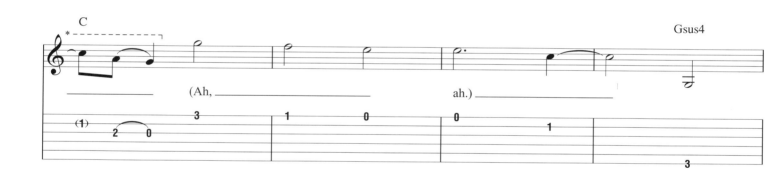

D.S. al Coda

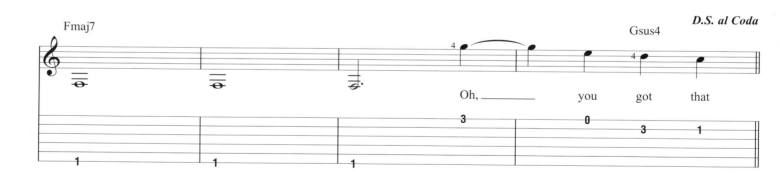

Coda

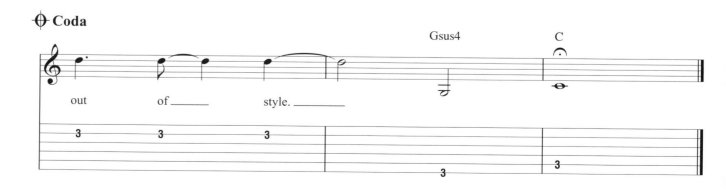

I Wish You Would

Words and Music by Taylor Swift and Jack Antonoff

Strum Pattern: 6
Pick Pattern: 4

Intro
Moderately, in 2

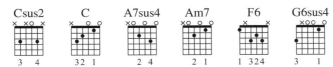

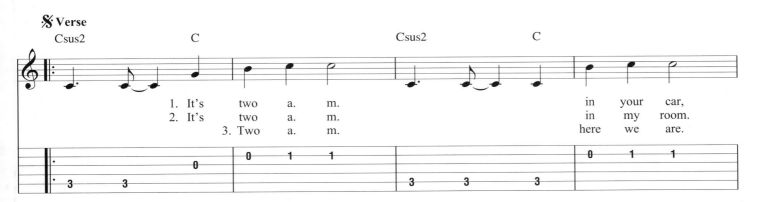

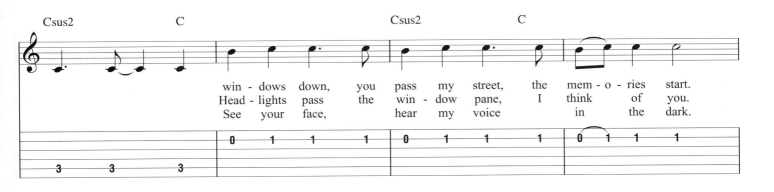

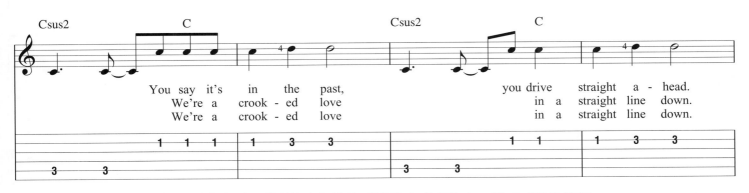

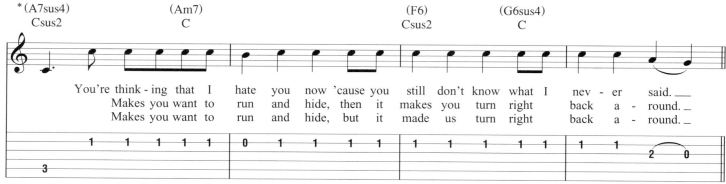

*(A7sus4)   *(Am7)*   *(F6)*   *(G6sus4)*
Csus2   C   Csus2   C

You're think-ing that I hate you now 'cause you still don't know what I nev-er said. ___
Makes you want to run and hide, then it makes you turn right back a-round. ___
Makes you want to run and hide, but it made us turn right back a-round. ___

*2nd & 3rd times, substitute chords in parentheses.

Chorus
Half-time feel

Csus2   C   Csus2   C

I wish you would come back, wish I nev-er hung up the phone ___ like I did, I

A7sus4   Am7   A7sus4   Am7

wish you knew that I'll nev-er for-get ___ you as long as I live, and I

3rd time, To Coda 1 ⊕
** **End half-time feel**

F6   G6sus4

wish you were right here, right now, it's all good, _____ I wish you would. __

**1st time only.

1.

Csus2   C   Csus2   C

I wish we could go back and re-mem-ber what we were fight - ing for, and I

wish you knew that I miss you too much_ to be mad an-y-more, and I

End half-time feel

wish you were right here, right now, it's all good,_____ I wish you would._

Interlude

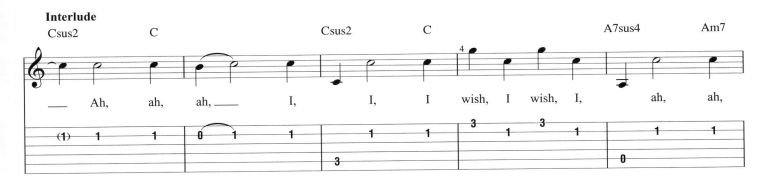

_ Ah, ah, ah,_____ I, I, I wish, I wish, I, ah, ah,

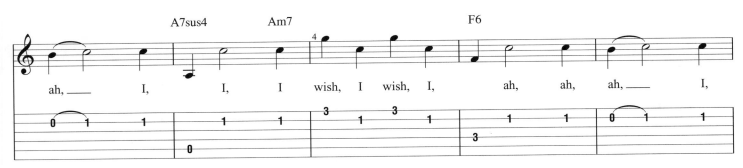

ah,_____ I, I, I wish, I wish, I, ah, ah, ah,_____ I,

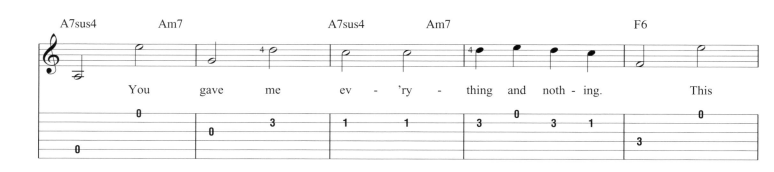

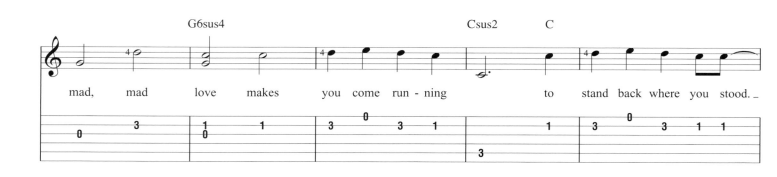

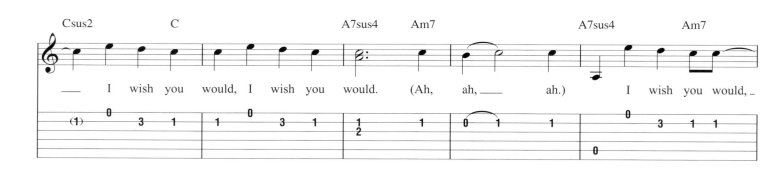

20

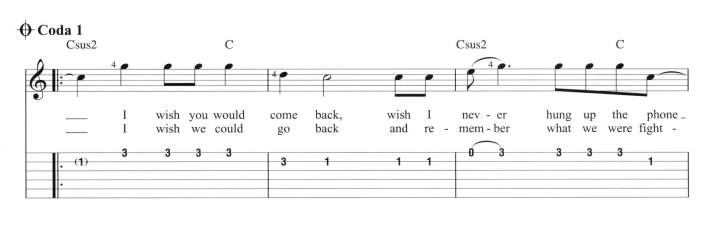

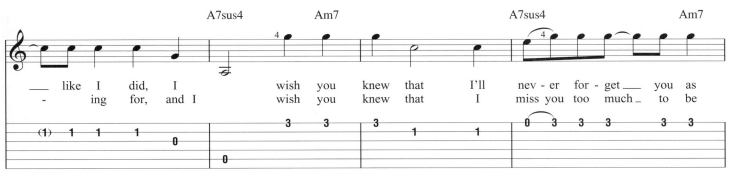

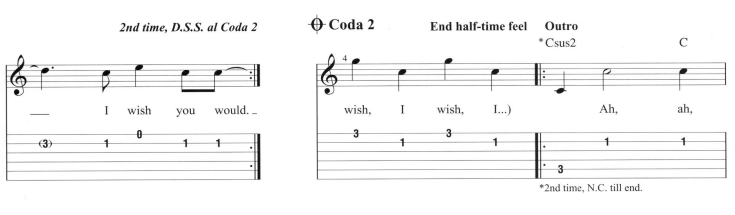

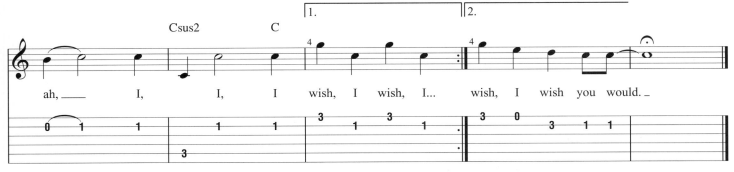

Out of the Woods

Words and Music by Taylor Swift and Jack Antonoff

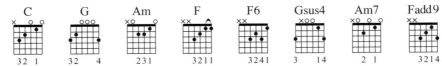

Strum Pattern: 3
Pick Pattern: 3

Intro
Moderately slow, in 2

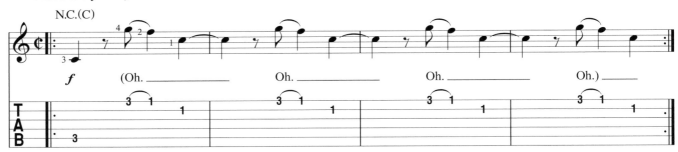

(Oh. _____ Oh. _____ Oh. _____ Oh.) _____

Verse

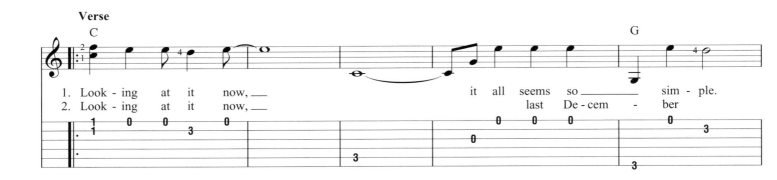

1. Look - ing at it now, _____ it all seems so _____ sim - ple.
2. Look - ing at it now, _____ last De - cem - ber

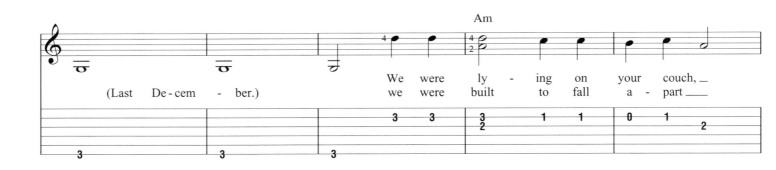

(Last De - cem - ber.) We were ly - ing on your couch, _____
we were built to fall a - part

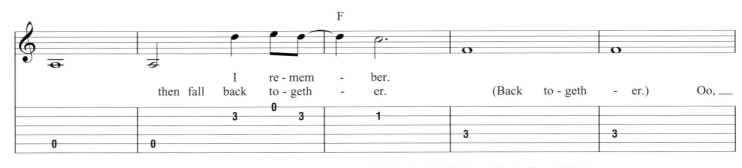

I re - mem - ber.
then fall back to - geth - er. (Back to - geth - er.) Oo, _____

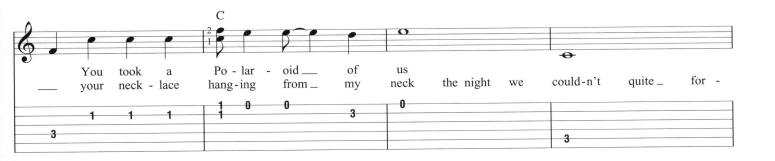

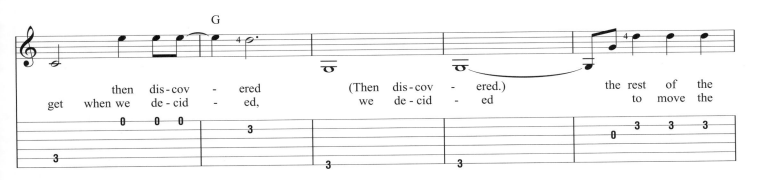

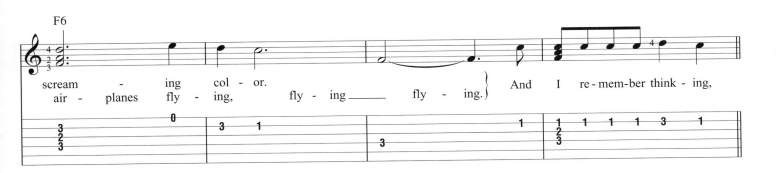

Chorus

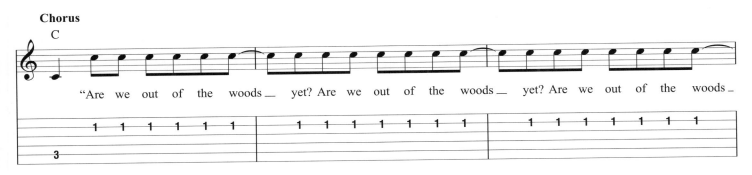

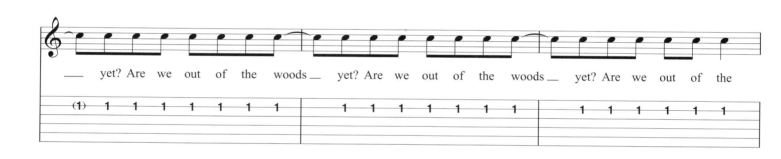

Interlude

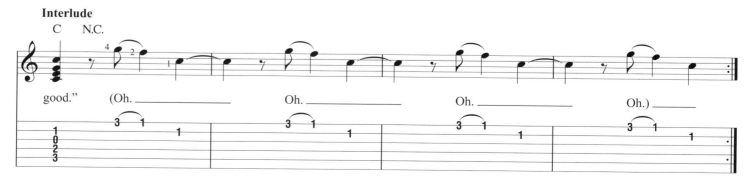

Bridge

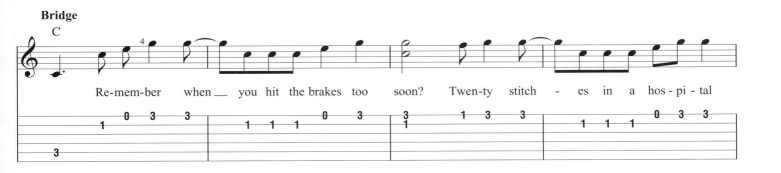

Re-mem-ber when ___ you hit the brakes too soon? Twen-ty stitch - es in a hos-pi-tal

room. When you start-ed cry - in', ba - by, I did too. But when the sun came

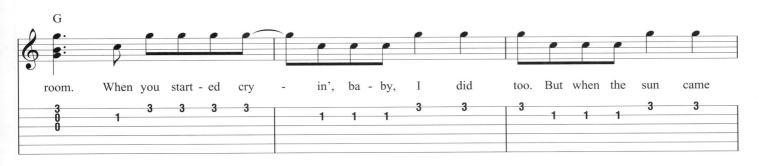

up I was look-in' at you. Re-mem-ber when ___ we could-n't take the heat? I walked out,___

___ I said, "I'm set-tin' you free." But the mon-sters turned ___ out to be just trees. When the sun came

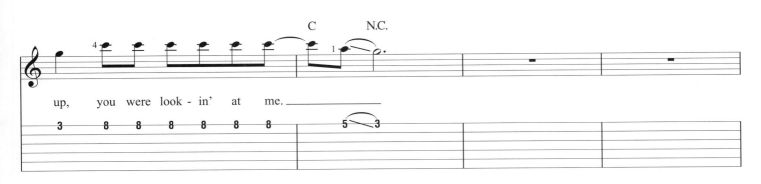

up, you were look - in' at me. _____

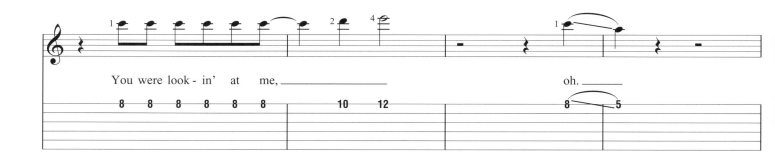

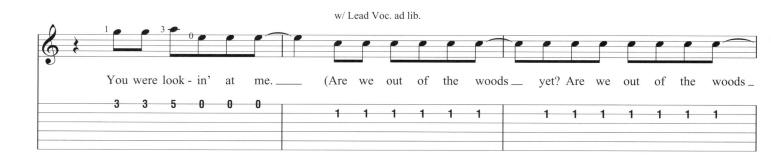

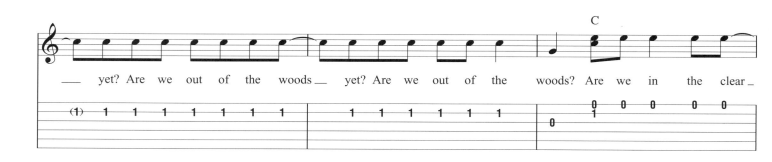

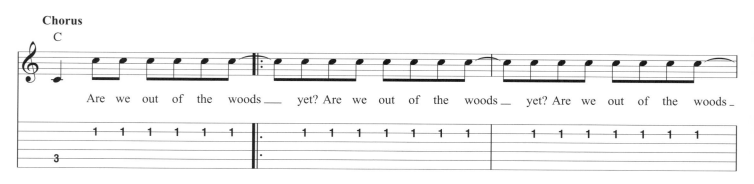

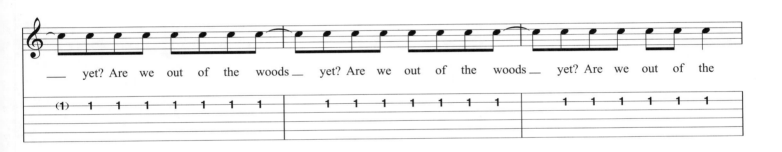

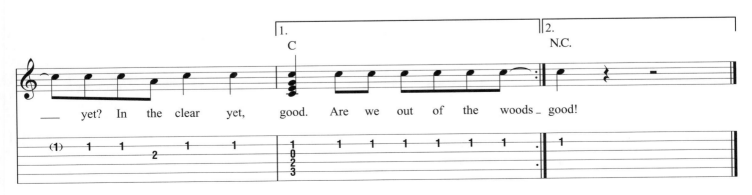

27

All You Had to Do Was Stay

Words and Music by Taylor Swift and Max Martin

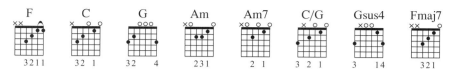

*Capo V

Strum Pattern: 5
Pick Pattern: 5

Verse
Moderately slow

*Optional: To match recording, place capo at 5th fret.

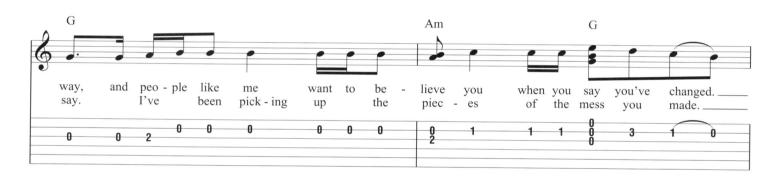

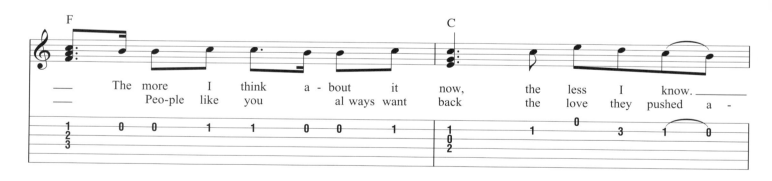

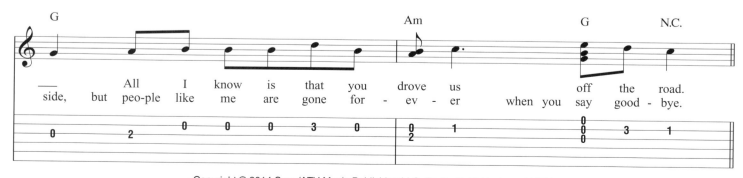

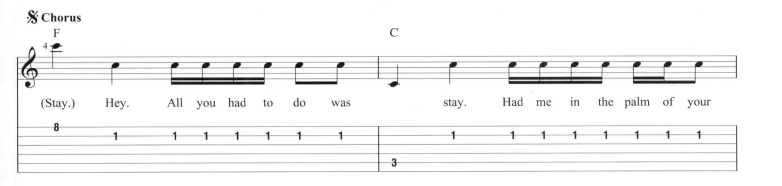

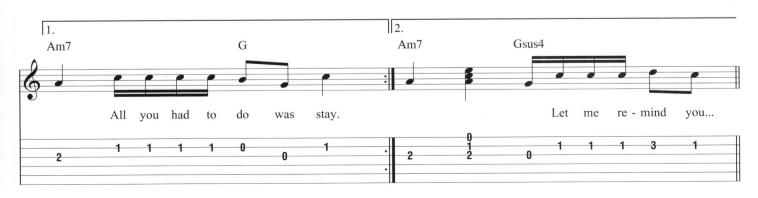

Bridge

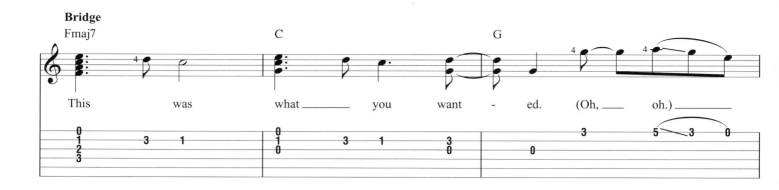

This was what _____ you want - ed. (Oh, _____ oh.) _____

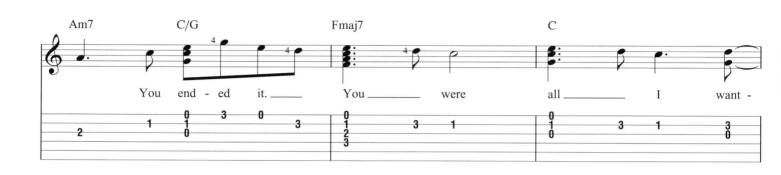

You end - ed it. _____ You _____ were all _____ I want -

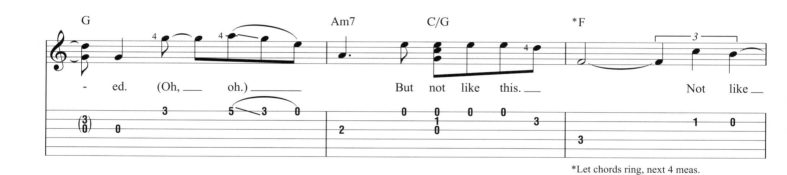

- ed. (Oh, _____ oh.) _____ But not like this. _____ Not like

*Let chords ring, next 4 meas.

D.S. al Coda

_____ this. _____ Not _____ like this. Oh, all you had to do was

Coda

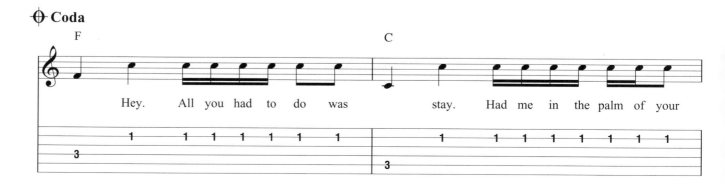

Hey. All you had to do was stay. Had me in the palm of your

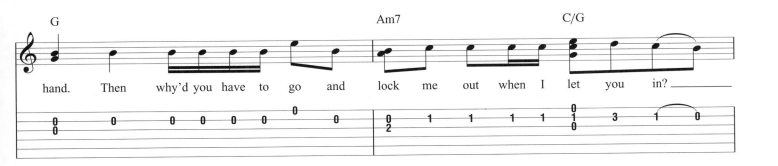

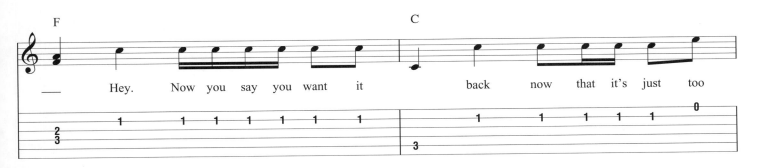

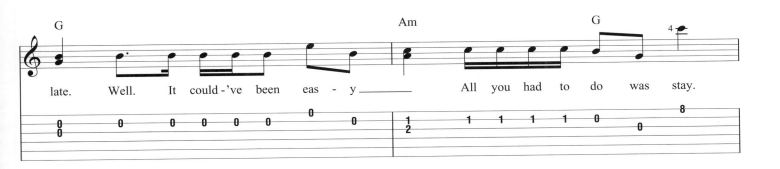

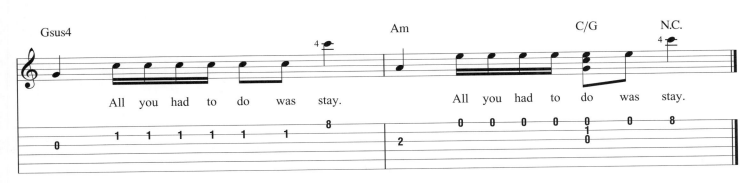

Shake It Off

Words and Music by Taylor Swift, Max Martin and Shellback

Strum Pattern: 3, 4
Pick Pattern: 4, 5

*Sung one octave higher.
**Chord symbols reflect implied harmony.

mm. That's what peo - ple say, _____ mm, mm. But I keep
mm. That's what they don't know, _____ mm, mm.

Pre-Chorus

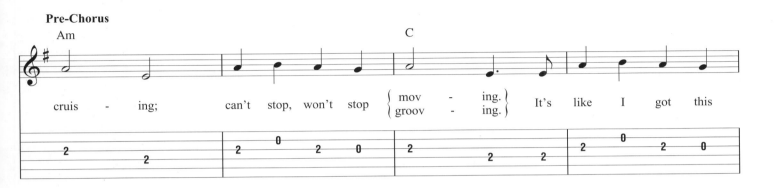

cruis - ing; can't stop, won't stop mov - ing. It's like I got this
groov - ing.

mu - sic in my mind say - ing, "It's gon - na be al - right." _ 'Cause the

*Sung as written.

𝄋 Chorus

play - ers gon - na play, play, play, play, play, and the hat - ers gon - na hate, hate,

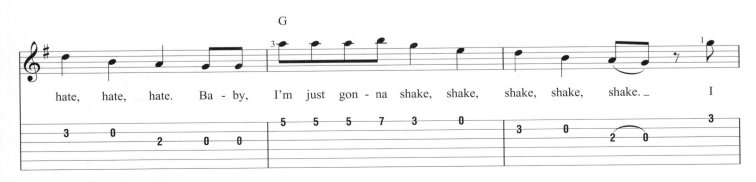

hate, hate, hate. Ba - by, I'm just gon - na shake, shake, shake, shake, shake. _ I

33

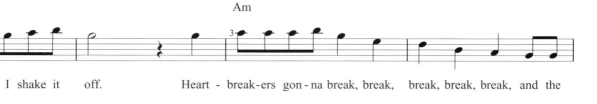

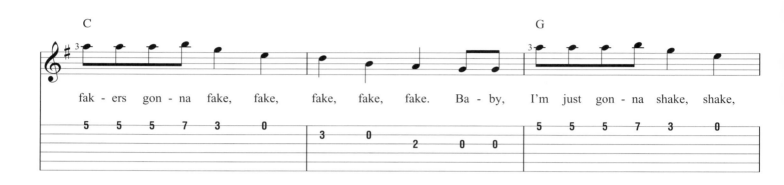

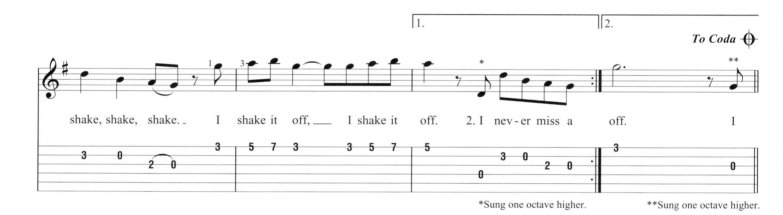

*Sung one octave higher.   **Sung one octave higher.

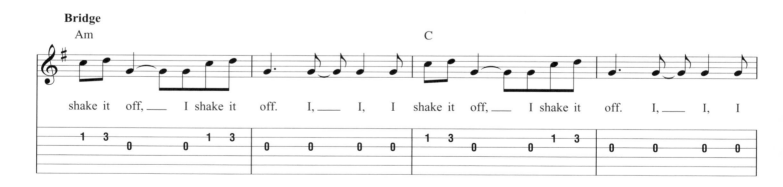

Bad Blood

Words and Music by Taylor Swift, Max Martin and Shellback

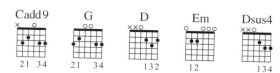

Strum Pattern: 6
Pick Pattern: 5

Chorus
Moderately slow

'Cause, ba-by, now we got bad ___ blood. You know it used to be mad ___ love. So take a

*Sung one octave higher.

look what you've done, ___ 'cause, ba-by, now we got bad ___ blood. *Hey!* Now we got prob - lems and I don't

**Shouted:

**Lyrics in italics are shouted throughout.

think we can solve ___ 'em. You made a real-ly deep cut. ___ And, ba-by, now we got bad ___ blood. *Hey!*

Verse

Cadd9   G   D   Em

1. Did you have to do this? I was think - in' that you could be trust - ed.
2. Did you think we'd be fine? Still got scars on my back from your knife, so

***Sung as written.

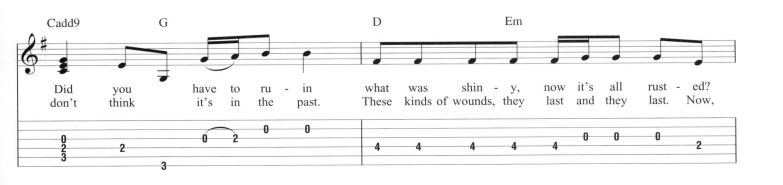

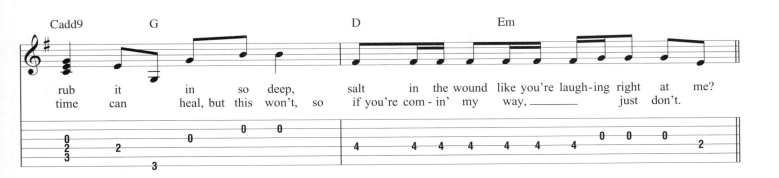

Pre-Chorus

*Sung one octave higher.

Chorus

look what you've done, ___ 'cause, ba-by, now we got bad ___ blood. *Hey!* Now we got prob - lems and I don't

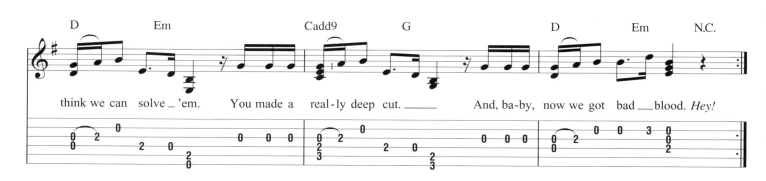

think we can solve _ 'em. You made a real-ly deep cut. ___ And, ba-by, now we got bad ___ blood. *Hey!*

Bridge

Band-aids don't fix bul - let holes. You say sor - ry just for show. If you live like that, you live with ghosts.

*Sung as written.

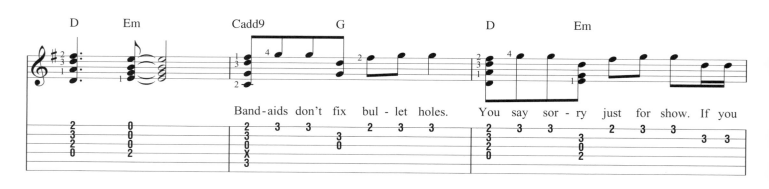

Band-aids don't fix bul - let holes. You say sor - ry just for show. If you

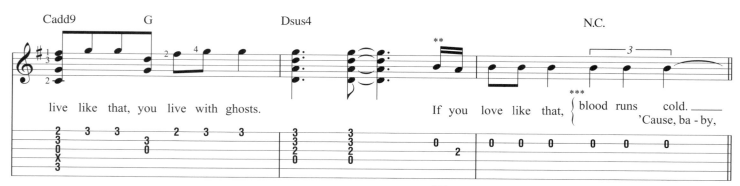

live like that, you live with ghosts. If you love like that, { blood runs cold. ___ 'Cause, ba - by,

**Sung one octave higher. ***Sung at once.

Chorus

Wildest Dreams

Words and Music by Taylor Swift, Max Martin and Shellback

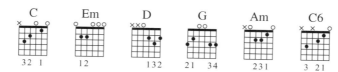

*Capo I

Strum Pattern: 4
Pick Pattern: 1

Intro
Moderately fast

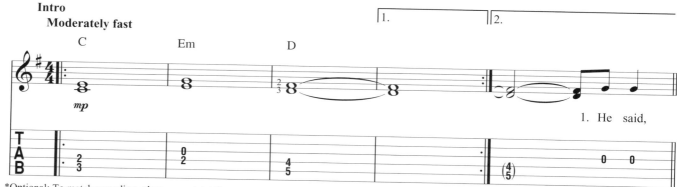

*Optional: To match recording, place capo at 1st fret.

Verse

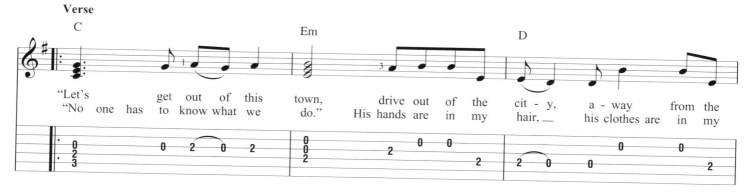

**Sung one octave higher.

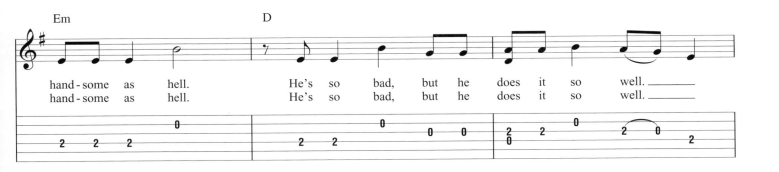

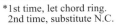
*1st time, let chord ring.
2nd time, substitute N.C.

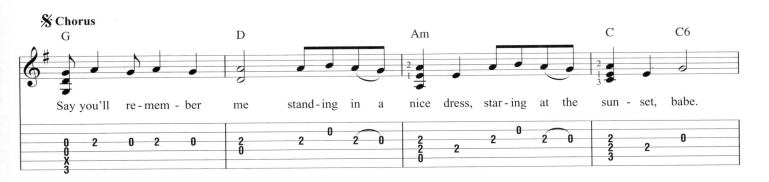

3rd time, To Coda ⊕

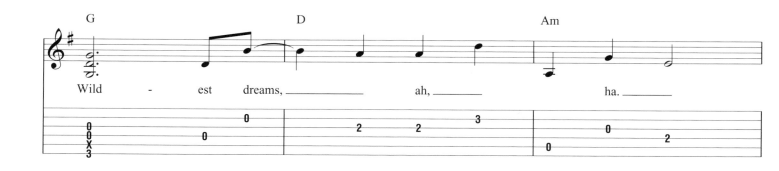

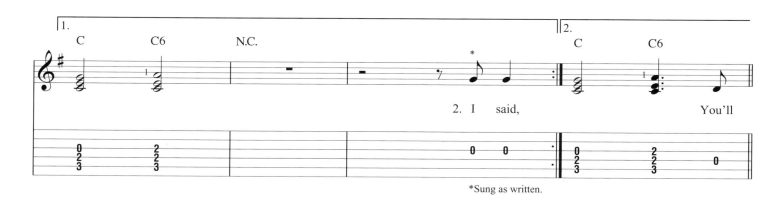

*Sung as written.

Bridge

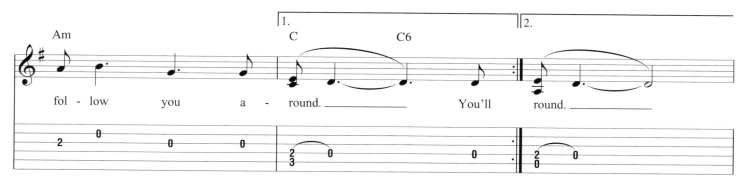

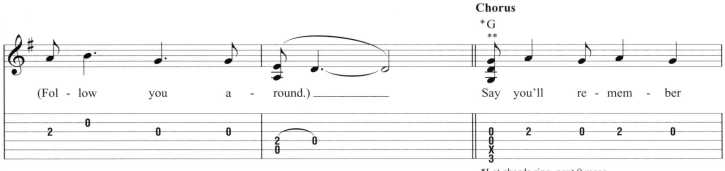

(Fol - low you a - round.) _____ Say you'll re - mem - ber

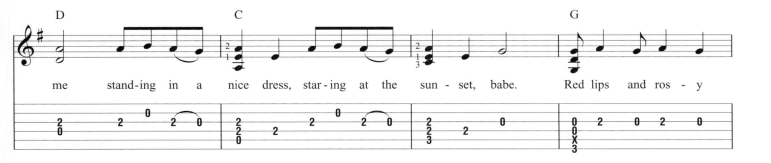

me stand-ing in a nice dress, star-ing at the sun - set, babe. Red lips and ros - y

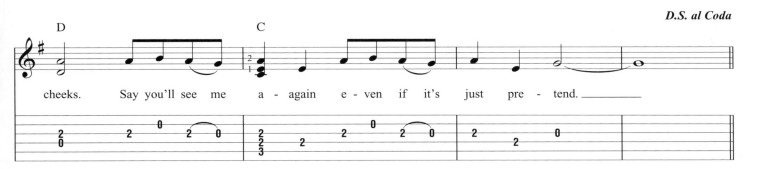

cheeks. Say you'll see me a - again e - ven if it's just pre - tend. _____

*Let chords ring, next 9 meas.
**Sung as written, next 9 meas.

D.S. al Coda

In your wild - est dreams, _____ ah, _____ ha. _____

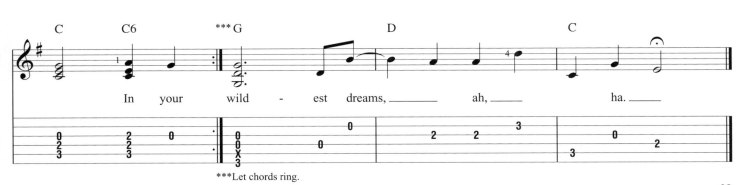

In your wild - est dreams, _____ ah, _____ ha. _____

***Let chords ring.

How You Get the Girl

Words and Music by Taylor Swift, Max Martin and Shellback

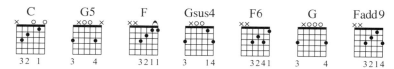

*Capo V

Strum Pattern: 2
Pick Pattern: 4

Intro
Moderately

*Optional: To match recording, place capo at 5th fret.

Verse

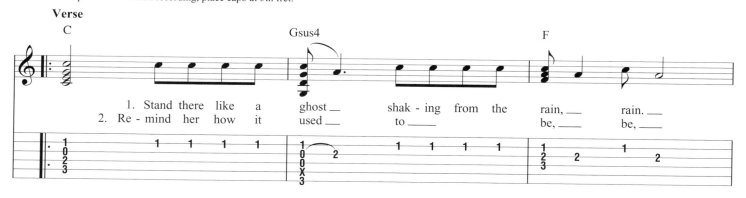

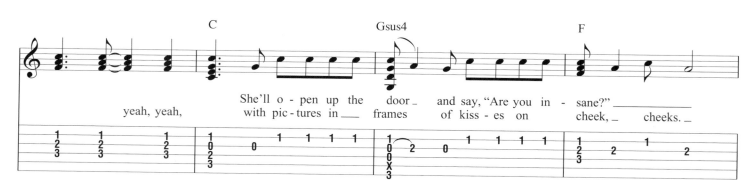

*Let chord ring.

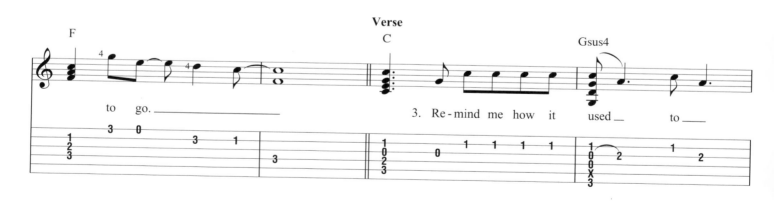

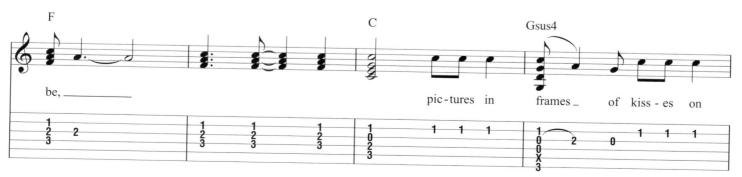

cheeks, _____ and say you want me, _____ yeah, _____ and then you say...

⊕ Coda

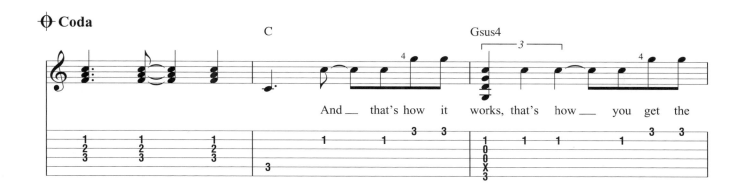

And __ that's how it works, that's how __ you get the

girl, _____ girl. _____ And __ that's how it

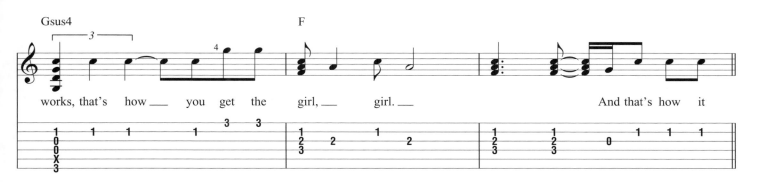

works, that's how __ you get the girl, _____ girl. _____ And that's how it

Outro

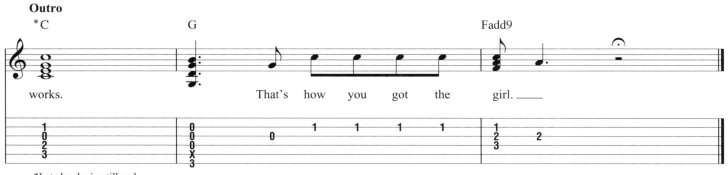

works. That's how you got the girl. _____

*Let chords ring till end.

This Love

Words and Music by Taylor Swift

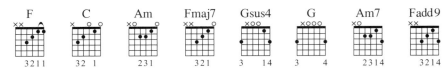

*Capo IV

Strum Pattern: 1
Pick Pattern: 5

Verse
Slow, in 2

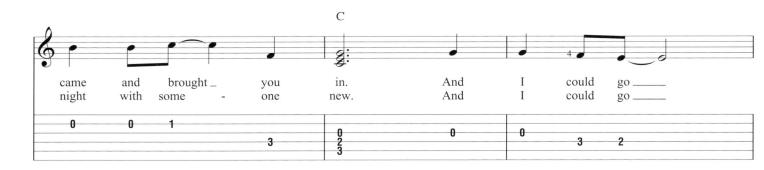

1. Clear blue ___ wa - ter, ___ high tide ___
2. Toss - ing, ___ turn - ing, ___ strug - gled through ___ the

*Optional: To match recording, place capo at 4th fret.

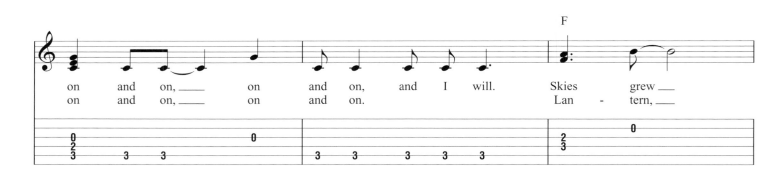

came and brought ___ you in. And I could go ___
night with some - one new. And I could go ___

on and on, ___ on and on, and I will. Skies grew ___
on and on, ___ on and on. Lan - tern, ___

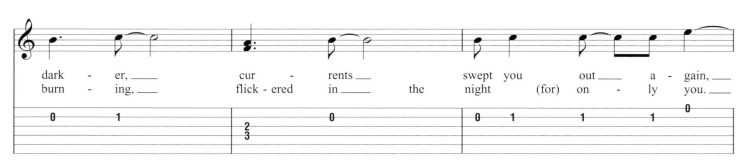

dark - er, ___ cur - rents ___ swept you out ___ a - gain,
burn - ing, ___ flick - ered in ___ the night (for) on - ly you.

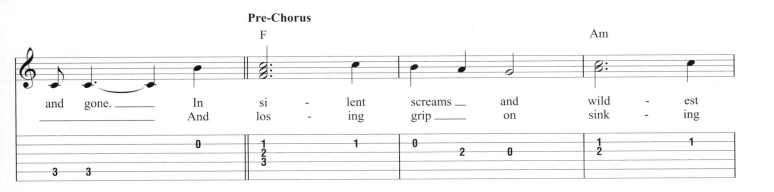

Pre-Chorus

𝄆 **Chorus**

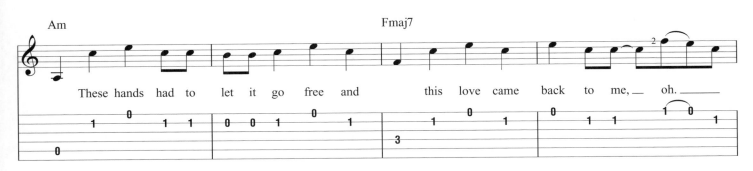

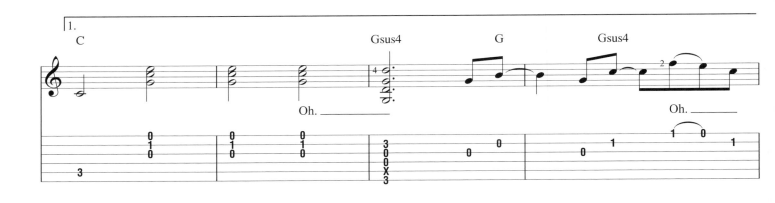

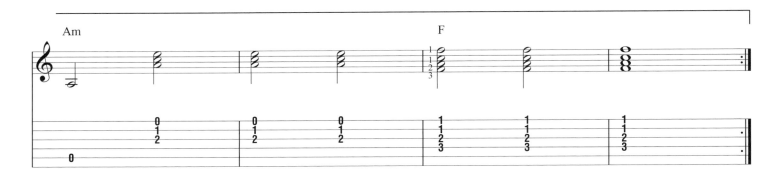

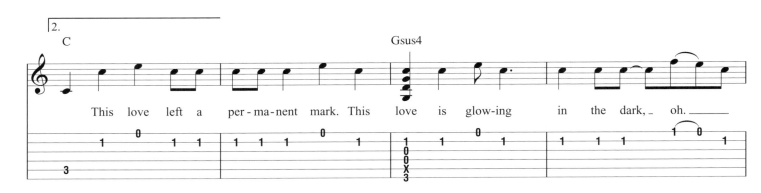

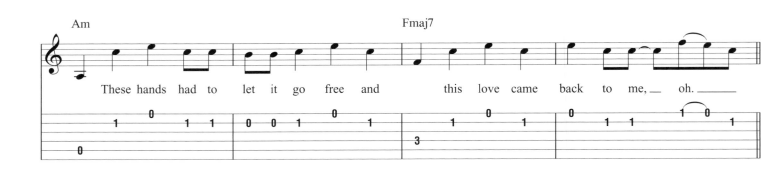

Interlude

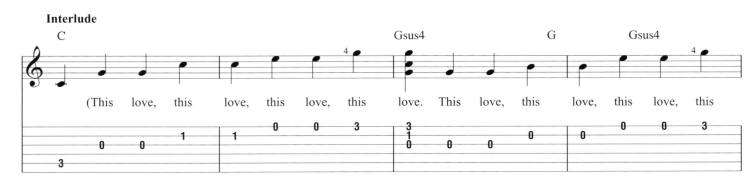

love. This love, this love, this love, this love. This love, this love, this love.) _____

Bridge

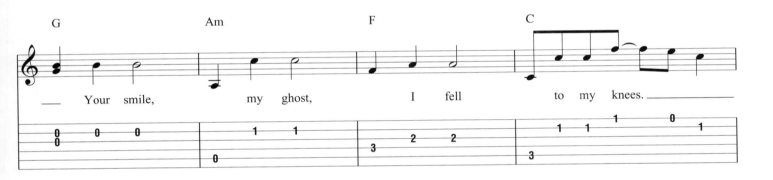

Your kiss, my cheek, I watched you leave. _____

___ Your smile, my ghost, I fell to my knees. _____

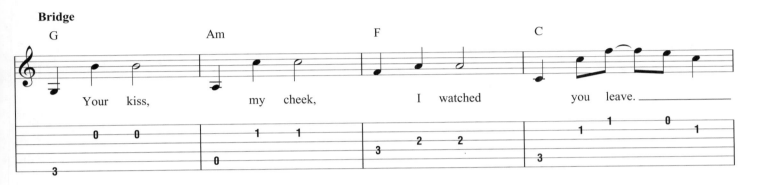

___ When you're young you just run, but you come back to what_ you need._

D.S. al Coda
(take 2nd ending)

⊕ **Coda**

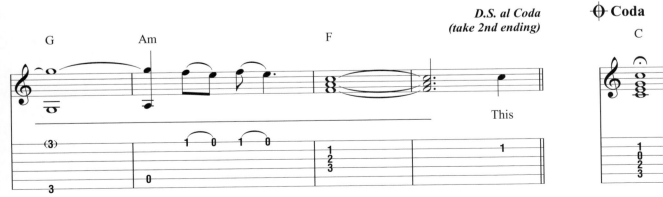

This

51

I Know Places

Words and Music by Taylor Swift and Ryan Tedder

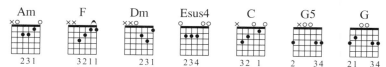

Strum Pattern: 1
Pick Pattern: 5

Intro
Moderately slow, in 2

*Chord symbols reflect implied harmony.

Verse

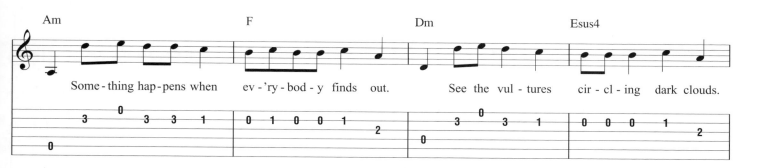

𝄋 Pre-Chorus

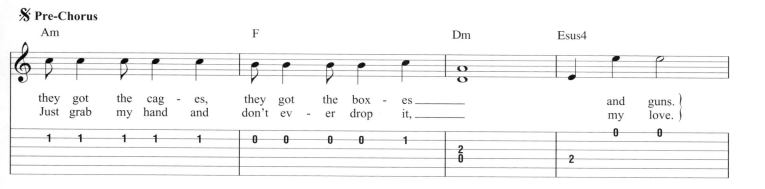

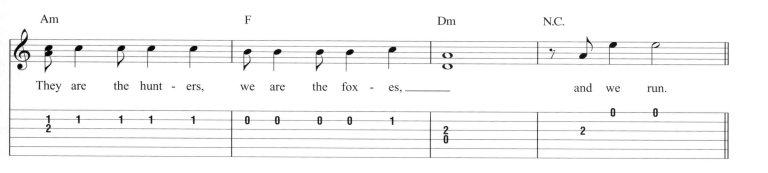

Chorus

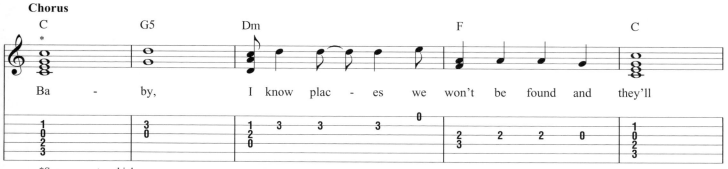

*Sung one octave higher.

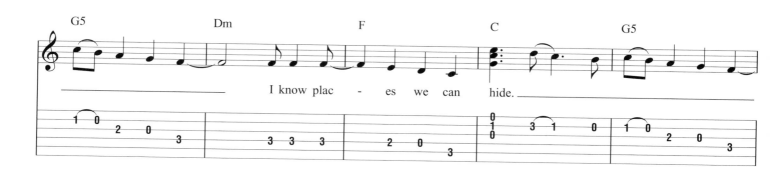

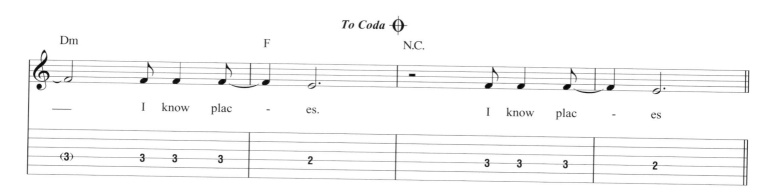

*Sung as written.

$\oplus$ Coda

Pre-Chorus

They are the hunt - ers, we are the fox - es, _____ and we run.

*Sung as written.

Just grab my hand and don't ev - er drop it, _____ my love.

Chorus

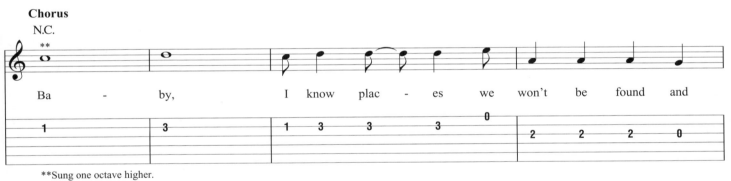

Ba - by, I know plac - es we won't be found and

**Sung one octave higher.

they'll be chas - ing their tails ___ try'n' to track us down 'cause

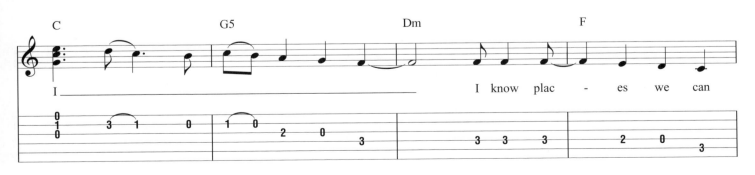

I _____ I know plac - es we can

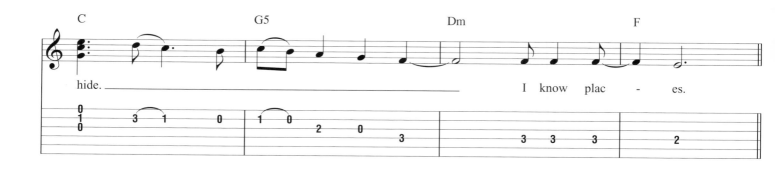

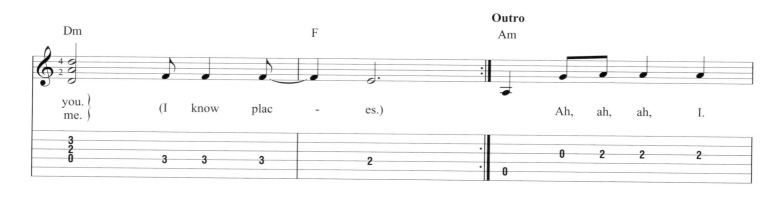

Clean

Words and Music by Taylor Swift and Imogen Heap

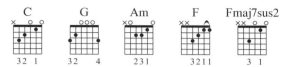

*Capo IV

Strum Pattern: 6
Pick Pattern: 5

Intro
Moderately

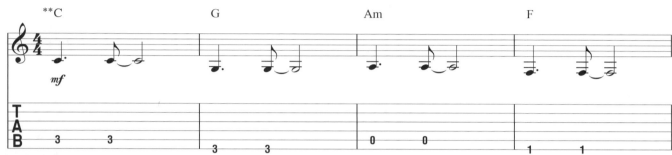

*Optional: To match recording, place capo at 4th fret.
**Chord symbols reflect implied harmony.

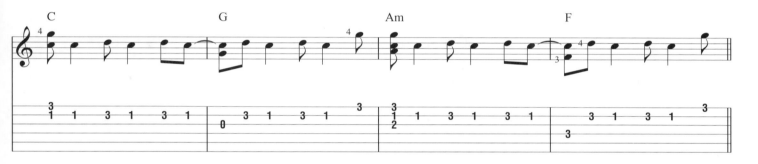

Verse

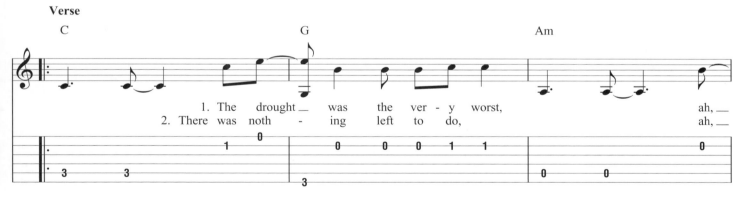

1. The drought ___ was the ver - y worst, ah, ___
2. There was noth - ing left to do, ah, ___

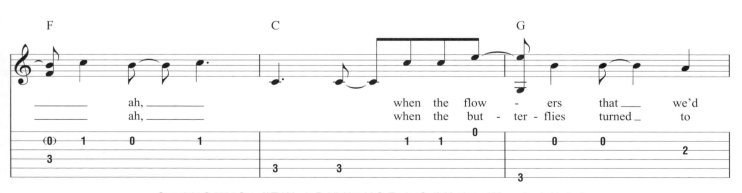

___ ah, ___ when the flow - ers that ___ we'd
___ ah, ___ when the but - ter - flies turned ___ to

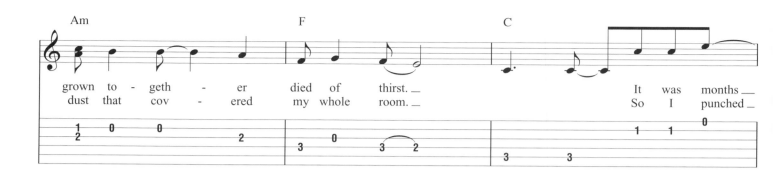

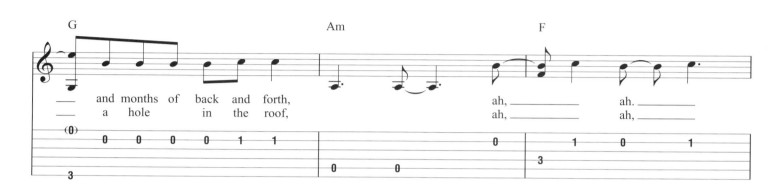

Chorus

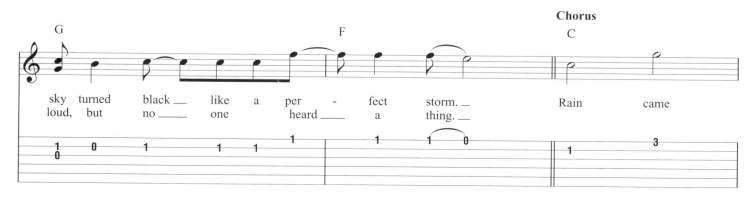

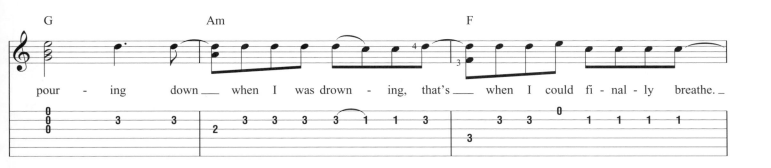

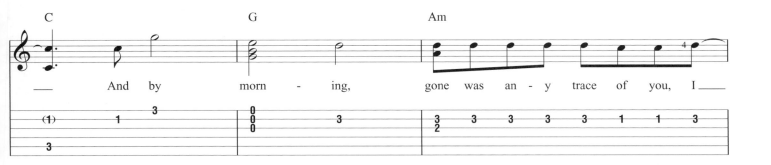

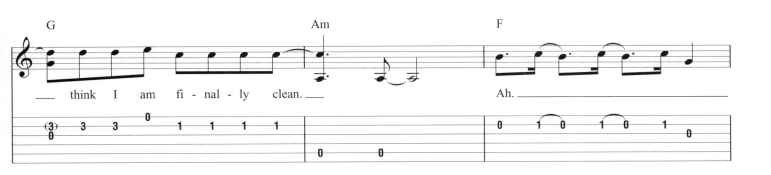

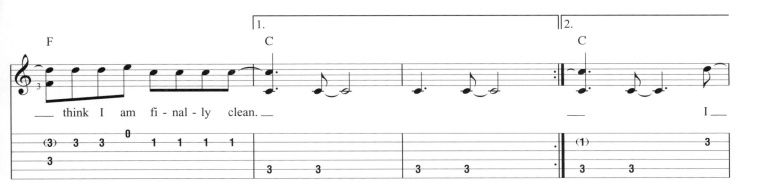

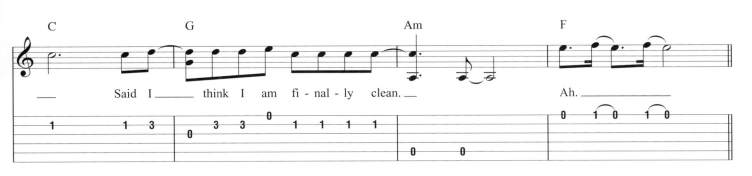

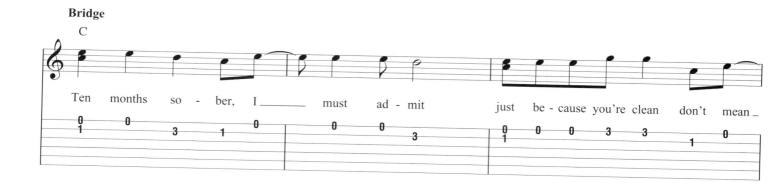

Bridge

Ten months so - ber, I _____ must ad - mit just be - cause you're clean don't mean _

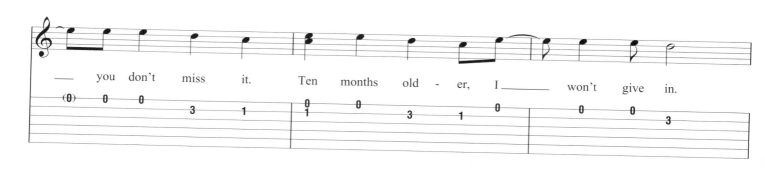

_____ you don't miss it. Ten months old - er, I _____ won't give in.

Now that I'm clean, I'm nev - er gon - na risk it. 3. The drought _ was the ver - y worst,

ah, _____ ah, _____ when the flow -

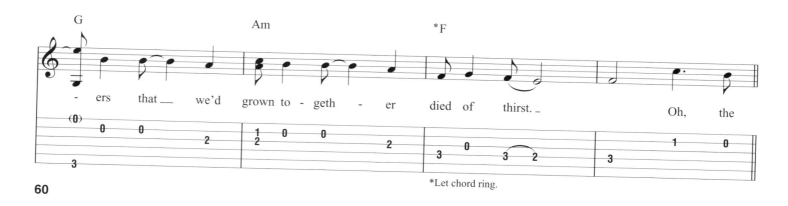

- ers that _ we'd grown to - geth - er died of thirst. _ Oh, the

*Let chord ring.

Chorus

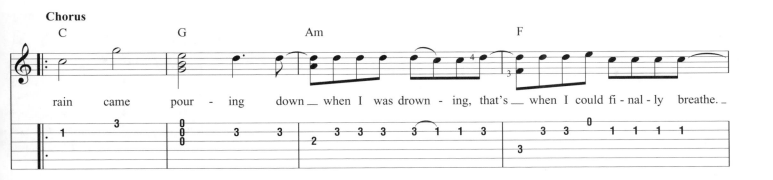

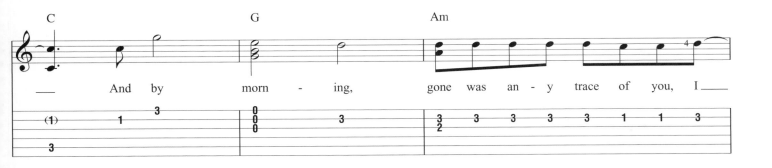

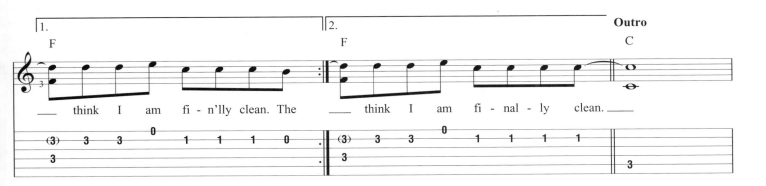

61

EASY GUITAR WITH NOTES & TAB

This series features simplified arrangements with notes, tab, chord charts, and strum and pick patterns.

MIXED FOLIOS

00702287	Acoustic	$14.99
00702002	Acoustic Rock Hits for Easy Guitar	$12.95
00702166	All-Time Best Guitar Collection	$19.99
00699665	Beatles Best	$12.95
00702232	Best Acoustic Songs for Easy Guitar	$12.99
00119835	Best Children's Songs	$16.99
00702233	Best Hard Rock Songs	$14.99
00703055	The Big Book of Nursery Rhymes & Children's Songs	$14.99
00322179	The Big Easy Book of Classic Rock Guitar	$24.95
00698978	Big Christmas Collection	$16.95
00702394	Bluegrass Songs for Easy Guitar	$12.99
00703387	Celtic Classics	$14.99
00125023	Chart Hits of 2013-2014	$14.99
00118314	Chart Hits of 2012-2013	$14.99
00702149	Children's Christian Songbook	$7.95
00702237	Christian Acoustic Favorites	$12.95
00702028	Christmas Classics	$7.95
00101779	Christmas Guitar	$14.99
00702185	Christmas Hits	$9.95
00702141	Classic Rock	$8.95
00702203	CMT's 100 Greatest Country Songs	$27.95
00702283	The Contemporary Christian Collection	$16.99
00702006	Contemporary Christian Favorites	$9.95
00702239	Country Classics for Easy Guitar	$19.99

00702282	Country Hits of 2009–2010	$14.99
00702240	Country Hits of 2007–2008	$12.95
00702085	Disney Movie Hits	$12.95
00702257	Easy Acoustic Guitar Songs	$14.99
00702280	Easy Guitar Tab White Pages	$29.99
00702212	Essential Christmas	$9.95
00702041	Favorite Hymns for Easy Guitar	$9.95
00702281	4 Chord Rock	$9.99
00126894	Frozen	$14.99
00702286	Glee	$16.99
00699374	Gospel Favorites	$14.95
00122138	The Grammy Awards® Record of the Year 1958-2011	$19.99
00702160	The Great American Country Songbook	$15.99
00702050	Great Classical Themes for Easy Guitar	$6.95
00702116	Greatest Hymns for Guitar	$8.95
00702130	The Groovy Years	$9.95
00702184	Guitar Instrumentals	$9.95
00702046	Hits of the '70s for Easy Guitar	$8.95
00702273	Irish Songs	$12.99
00702275	Jazz Favorites for Easy Guitar	$14.99
00702274	Jazz Standards for Easy Guitar	$14.99
00702162	Jumbo Easy Guitar Songbook	$19.95
00702258	Legends of Rock	$14.99
00702261	Modern Worship Hits	$14.99
00702189	MTV's 100 Greatest Pop Songs	$24.95

00702272	1950s Rock	$14
00702271	1960s Rock	$14
00702270	1970s Rock	$14
00702269	1980s Rock	$14
00702268	1990s Rock	$14
00109725	Once	$14
00702187	Selections from O Brother Where Art Thou?	$12
00702178	100 Songs for Kids	$12
00702515	Pirates of the Caribbean	$12
00702125	Praise and Worship for Guitar	$9
00702155	Rock Hits for Guitar	$9
00702285	Southern Rock Hits	$12
00702866	Theme Music	$12
00121535	30 Easy Celtic Guitar Solos	$14
00702220	Today's Country Hits	$9
00702198	Today's Hits for Guitar	$9
00121900	Today's Women of Pop & Rock	$14
00702217	Top Christian Hits	$12
00702235	Top Christian Hits of '07–'08	$14
00103626	Top Hits of 2012	$14
00702294	Top Worship Hits	$14
00702206	Very Best of Rock	$9
00702255	VH1's 100 Greatest Hard Rock Songs	$27
00702175	VH1's 100 Greatest Songs of Rock and Roll	$24
00702253	Wicked	$12

ARTIST COLLECTIONS

00702267	AC/DC for Easy Guitar	$15.99
00702598	Adele for Easy Guitar	$14.99
00702001	Best of Aerosmith	$16.95
00702040	Best of the Allman Brothers	$14.99
00702865	J.S. Bach for Easy Guitar	$12.99
00702169	Best of The Beach Boys	$12.99
00702292	The Beatles — 1	$19.99
00125796	Best of Chuck Berry	$14.99
00702201	The Essential Black Sabbath	$12.95
02501615	Zac Brown Band — The Foundation	$16.99
02501621	Zac Brown Band — You Get What You Give	$16.99
00702043	Best of Johnny Cash	$16.99
00702291	Very Best of Coldplay	$12.99
00702263	Best of Casting Crowns	$12.99
00702090	Eric Clapton's Best	$10.95
00702086	Eric Clapton — from the Album Unplugged	$10.95
00702202	The Essential Eric Clapton	$12.95
00702250	blink-182 — Greatest Hits	$12.99
00702053	Best of Patsy Cline	$10.95
00702229	The Very Best of Creedence Clearwater Revival	$14.99
00702145	Best of Jim Croce	$14.99
00702278	Crosby, Stills & Nash	$12.99
00702219	David Crowder*Band Collection	$12.95
00702276	Fleetwood Mac — Easy Guitar Collection	$14.99
00702136	Best of Merle Haggard	$12.99
00702227	Jimi Hendrix — Smash Hits	$14.99

00702288	Best of Hillsong United	$12.99
00702236	Best of Antonio Carlos Jobim	$12.95
00702245	Elton John — Greatest Hits 1970–2002	$14.99
00129855	Jack Johnson	$14.99
00702204	Robert Johnson	$9.95
00702234	Selections from Toby Keith — 35 Biggest Hits	$12.95
00702003	Kiss	$9.95
00110578	Best of Kutless	$12.99
00702216	Lynyrd Skynyrd	$15.99
00702182	The Essential Bob Marley	$12.95
00702346	Bruno Mars — Doo-Wops & Hooligans	$12.99
00121925	Bruno Mars – Unorthodox Jukebox	$12.99
00702248	Paul McCartney — All the Best	$14.99
00702129	Songs of Sarah McLachlan	$12.95
02501316	Metallica — Death Magnetic	$15.95
00702209	Steve Miller Band — Young Hearts (Greatest Hits)	$12.95
00124167	Jason Mraz	$14.99
00702096	Best of Nirvana	$14.95
00702211	The Offspring — Greatest Hits	$12.95
00702030	Best of Roy Orbison	$12.95
00702144	Best of Ozzy Osbourne	$14.99
00702279	Tom Petty	$12.99
00102911	Pink Floyd	$16.99
00702139	Elvis Country Favorites	$9.95
00702293	The Very Best of Prince	$12.99
00699415	Best of Queen for Guitar	$14.99

00109279	Best of R.E.M.	$14.
00702208	Red Hot Chili Peppers — Greatest Hits	$12.
00702093	Rolling Stones Collection	$17.
00702196	Best of Bob Seger	$12.
00702252	Frank Sinatra — Nothing But the Best	$12.
00702010	Best of Rod Stewart	$14.
00702049	Best of George Strait	$12.
00702259	Taylor Swift for Easy Guitar	$14.
00702260	Taylor Swift – Fearless	$12.
00115960	Taylor Swift — Red	$16.
00702290	Taylor Swift — Speak Now	$15.
00702262	Chris Tomlin Collection	$14.
00702226	Chris Tomlin — See the Morning	$12.
00702427	U2 — 18 Singles	$14.
00702108	Best of Stevie Ray Vaughan	$10.
00702123	Best of Hank Williams	$12.
00702111	Stevie Wonder — Guitar Collection	$9.
00702228	Neil Young — Greatest Hits	$15.
00119133	Neil Young – Harvest	$14.
00702188	Essential ZZ Top	$10.

Prices, contents and availability subject to change without notice.

7777 W. BLUEMOUND RD. P.O. BOX 13819 MILWAUKEE, WI 53213

Visit Hal Leonard online at
www.halleonard.com

08

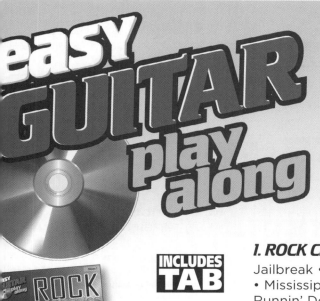

easy GUITAR play along

INCLUDES TAB

The *easy Guitar play along*® Series features streamlined transcriptions of your favorite songs. Just follow the tab, listen to the CD to hear how the guitar should sound, and then play along using the backing tracks. The CD is playable on any CD player, and is also enhanced to include the Amazing Slowdowner technology so Mac and PC users can adjust the recording to any tempo without changing the pitch!

1. ROCK CLASSICS
Jailbreak • Living After Midnight • Mississippi Queen • Rocks Off • Runnin' Down a Dream • Smoke on the Water • Strutter • Up Around the Bend.
00702560 Book/CD Pack.......$14.99

2. ACOUSTIC TOP HITS
About a Girl • I'm Yours • The Lazy Song • The Scientist • 21 Guns • Upside Down • What I Got • Wonderwall.
00702569 Book/CD Pack.......$14.99

3. ROCK HITS
All the Small Things • Best of You • Brain Stew (The Godzilla Remix) • Californication • Island in the Sun • Plush • Smells like Teen Spirit • Use Somebody.
00702570 Book/CD Pack.......$14.99

4. ROCK 'N' ROLL
Blue Suede Shoes • I Get Around • I'm a Believer • Jailhouse Rock • Oh, Pretty Woman • Peggy Sue • Runaway • Wake up Little Susie.
00702572 Book/CD Pack.....$14.99

5. ULTIMATE ACOUSTIC
Against the Wind • Babe, I'm Gonna Leave You • Come Monday • Free Fallin' • Give a Little Bit • Have You Ever Seen the Rain? • New Kid in Town • We Can Work It Out.
00702573 Book/CD Pack........$14.99

6. CHRISTMAS SONGS
Have Yourself a Merry Little Christmas • A Holly Jolly Christmas • The Little Drummer Boy • Run Rudolph Run • Santa Claus Is Comin' to Town • Silver and Gold • Sleigh Ride • Winter Wonderland.
00101879 Book/CD Pack.........$14.99

7. BLUES SONGS FOR BEGINNERS
Come On (Part 1) • Double Trouble • Gangster of Love • I'm Ready • Let Me Love You Baby • Mary Had a Little Lamb • San-Ho-Zay • T-Bone Shuffle.
00103235 Book/CD Pack.....$14.99

8. ACOUSTIC SONGS FOR BEGINNERS
Barely Breathing • Drive • Everlong • Good Riddance (Time of Your Life) • Hallelujah • Hey There Delilah • Lake of Fire • Photograph.
00103240 Book/CD Pack.....$14.99

9. ROCK SONGS FOR BEGINNERS
Are You Gonna Be My Girl • Buddy Holly • Everybody Hurts • In Bloom • Otherside • The Rock Show • Santa Monica • When I Come Around.
00103255 Book/CD Pack.....$14.99

10. GREEN DAY
Basket Case • Boulevard of Broken Dreams • Good Riddance (Time of Your Life) • Holiday • Longview • 21 Guns • Wake Me up When September Ends • When I Come Around.
00122322 Book/CD Pack $14.99

11. NIRVANA
All Apologies • Come As You Are • Heart Shaped Box • Lake of Fire • Lithium • The Man Who Sold the World • Rape Me • Smells like Teen Spirit.
00122325 Book/CD Pack $14.99

12. TAYLOR SWIFT
Fifteen • Love Story • Mean • Picture to Burn • Red • We Are Never Ever Getting Back Together • White Horse • You Belong with Me.
00122326 Book/CD Pack $16.99

HAL•LEONARD® CORPORATION
77 W. BLUEMOUND RD. P.O. BOX 13819 MILWAUKEE, WI 53213

www.halleonard.com

Prices, contents, and availability subject to change without notice.

0214

HAL•LEONARD GUITAR PLAY-ALONG

This series will help you play your favorite songs quickly and easily. Just follow the tab and listen to the CD to the hear how the guitar should sound, and then play along using the separate backing tracks. Mac or PC users can also slow down the tempo without changing pitch by using the CD in their computer. The melody and lyrics are included in the book so that you can sing or simply follow along.

INCLUDES TAB

VOL. 1 – ROCK	00699570 / $16.99	
VOL. 2 – ACOUSTIC	00699569 / $16.95	
VOL. 3 – HARD ROCK	00699573 / $16.95	
VOL. 4 – POP/ROCK	00699571 / $16.99	
VOL. 5 – MODERN ROCK	00699574 / $16.99	
VOL. 6 – '90S ROCK	00699572 / $16.99	
VOL. 7 – BLUES	00699575 / $16.95	
VOL. 8 – ROCK	00699585 / $14.99	
VOL. 9 – PUNK ROCK	00699576 / $14.95	
VOL. 10 – ACOUSTIC	00699586 / $16.95	
VOL. 11 – EARLY ROCK	00699579 / $14.95	
VOL. 12 – POP/ROCK	00699587 / $14.95	
VOL. 13 – FOLK ROCK	00699581 / $15.99	
VOL. 14 – BLUES ROCK	00699582 / $16.95	
VOL. 15 – R&B	00699583 / $14.95	
VOL. 16 – JAZZ	00699584 / $15.95	
VOL. 17 – COUNTRY	00699588 / $15.95	
VOL. 18 – ACOUSTIC ROCK	00699577 / $15.95	
VOL. 19 – SOUL	00699578 / $14.99	
VOL. 20 – ROCKABILLY	00699580 / $14.95	
VOL. 21 – YULETIDE	00699602 / $14.95	
VOL. 22 – CHRISTMAS	00699600 / $15.95	
VOL. 23 – SURF	00699635 / $14.95	
VOL. 24 – ERIC CLAPTON	00699649 / $17.99	
VOL. 25 – LENNON & MCCARTNEY	00699642 / $16.99	
VOL. 26 – ELVIS PRESLEY	00699643 / $14.95	
VOL. 27 – DAVID LEE ROTH	00699645 / $16.95	
VOL. 28 – GREG KOCH	00699646 / $14.95	
VOL. 29 – BOB SEGER	00699647 / $15.99	
VOL. 30 – KISS	00699644 / $16.99	
VOL. 31 – CHRISTMAS HITS	00699652 / $14.95	
VOL. 32 – THE OFFSPRING	00699653 / $14.95	
VOL. 33 – ACOUSTIC CLASSICS	00699656 / $16.95	
VOL. 34 – CLASSIC ROCK	00699658 / $16.95	
VOL. 35 – HAIR METAL	00699660 / $16.95	
VOL. 36 – SOUTHERN ROCK	00699661 / $16.95	
VOL. 37 – ACOUSTIC UNPLUGGED	00699662 / $22.99	
VOL. 38 – BLUES	00699663 / $16.95	
VOL. 39 – '80S METAL	00699664 / $16.99	
VOL. 40 – INCUBUS	00699668 / $17.95	
VOL. 41 – ERIC CLAPTON	00699669 / $16.95	
VOL. 42 – 2000S ROCK	00699670 / $16.99	
VOL. 43 – LYNYRD SKYNYRD	00699681 / $17.95	
VOL. 44 – JAZZ	00699689 / $14.99	
VOL. 45 – TV THEMES	00699718 / $14.95	
VOL. 46 – MAINSTREAM ROCK	00699722 / $16.95	
VOL. 47 – HENDRIX SMASH HITS	00699723 / $19.95	
VOL. 48 – AEROSMITH CLASSICS	00699724 / $17.99	
VOL. 49 – STEVIE RAY VAUGHAN	00699725 / $17.99	
VOL. 51 – ALTERNATIVE '90S	00699727 / $14.99	
VOL. 52 – FUNK	00699728 / $14.95	
VOL. 53 – DISCO	00699729 / $14.99	
VOL. 54 – HEAVY METAL	00699730 / $14.95	
VOL. 55 – POP METAL	00699731 / $14.95	
VOL. 56 – FOO FIGHTERS	00699749 / $15.99	
VOL. 57 – SYSTEM OF A DOWN	00699751 / $14.95	
VOL. 58 – BLINK-182	00699772 / $14.95	
VOL. 59 – CHET ATKINS	00702347 / $16.99	
VOL. 60 – 3 DOORS DOWN	00699774 / $14.95	
VOL. 61 – SLIPKNOT	00699775 / $16.99	
VOL. 62 – CHRISTMAS CAROLS	00699798 / $12.95	
VOL. 63 – CREEDENCE CLEARWATER REVIVAL	00699802 / $16.99	
VOL. 64 – THE ULTIMATE OZZY OSBOURNE	00699803 / $16.99	
VOL. 66 – THE ROLLING STONES	00699807 / $16.95	
VOL. 67 – BLACK SABBATH	00699808 / $16.99	
VOL. 68 – PINK FLOYD – DARK SIDE OF THE MOON	00699809 / $16.99	
VOL. 69 – ACOUSTIC FAVORITES	00699810 / $14.95	
VOL. 70 – OZZY OSBOURNE	00699805 / $16.99	
VOL. 71 – CHRISTIAN ROCK	00699824 / $14.95	
VOL. 73 – BLUESY ROCK	00699829 / $16.99	
VOL. 75 – TOM PETTY	00699882 / $16.99	
VOL. 76 – COUNTRY HITS	00699884 / $14.95	
VOL. 77 – BLUEGRASS	00699910 / $14.99	
VOL. 78 – NIRVANA	00700132 / $16.99	
VOL. 79 – NEIL YOUNG	00700133 / $24.99	
VOL. 80 – ACOUSTIC ANTHOLOGY	00700175 / $19.95	
VOL. 81 – ROCK ANTHOLOGY	00700176 / $22.99	
VOL. 82 – EASY SONGS	00700177 / $12.99	
VOL. 83 – THREE CHORD SONGS	00700178 / $16.99	
VOL. 84 – STEELY DAN	00700200 / $16.99	
VOL. 85 – THE POLICE	00700269 /$16.99	
VOL. 86 – BOSTON	00700465 / $16.99	
VOL. 87 – ACOUSTIC WOMEN	00700763 / $14.99	
VOL. 88 – GRUNGE	00700467 / $16.99	
VOL. 89 – REGGAE	00700468 / $15.99	
VOL. 90 – CLASSICAL POP	00700469 / $14.99	
VOL. 91 – BLUES INSTRUMENTALS	00700505 / $14.99	
VOL. 92 – EARLY ROCK INSTRUMENTALS	00700506 / $14.99	
VOL. 93 – ROCK INSTRUMENTALS	00700507 / $16.99	
VOL. 95 – BLUES CLASSICS	00700509 / $14.99	
VOL. 96 – THIRD DAY	00700560 / $14.95	
VOL. 97 – ROCK BAND	00700703 / $14.99	
VOL. 99 – ZZ TOP	00700762 / $16.99	
VOL. 100 – B.B. KING	00700466 / $16.99	
VOL. 101 – SONGS FOR BEGINNERS	00701917 / $14.99	
VOL. 102 – CLASSIC PUNK	00700769 / $14.99	
VOL. 103 – SWITCHFOOT	00700773 / $16.99	
VOL. 104 – DUANE ALLMAN	00700846 / $16.99	
VOL. 106 – WEEZER	00700958 / $14.99	
VOL. 107 – CREAM	00701069 / $16.99	
VOL. 108 – THE WHO	00701053 / $16.99	
VOL. 109 – STEVE MILLER	00701054 / $14.99	
VOL. 111 – JOHN MELLENCAMP	00701056 / $14.99	
VOL. 112 – QUEEN	00701052 / $16.99	
VOL. 113 – JIM CROCE	00701058 / $15.99	
VOL. 114 – BON JOVI	00701060 / $14.99	
VOL. 115 – JOHNNY CASH	00701070 / $14.99	
VOL. 116 – THE VENTURES	00701124 / $14.99	
VOL. 117 – BRAD PAISLEY	00701224/ $16.99	
VOL. 118 – ERIC JOHNSON	00701353 / $16.99	
VOL. 119 – AC/DC CLASSICS	00701356 / $1
VOL. 120 – PROGRESSIVE ROCK	00701457 / $1
VOL. 121 – U2	00701508 / $1
VOL. 123 – LENNON & MCCARTNEY ACOUSTIC	00701614 / $1
VOL. 124 – MODERN WORSHIP	00701629 / $1
VOL. 125 – JEFF BECK	00701687 / $1
VOL. 126 – BOB MARLEY	00701701 / $1
VOL. 127 – 1970S ROCK	00701739 / $1
VOL. 128 – 1960S ROCK	00701740 / $1
VOL. 129 – MEGADETH	00701741 / $1
VOL. 131 – 1990S ROCK	00701743 / $1
VOL. 132 – COUNTRY ROCK	00701757 / $1
VOL. 133 – TAYLOR SWIFT	00701894 / $1
VOL. 134 – AVENGED SEVENFOLD	00701906 / $1
VOL. 136 – GUITAR THEMES	00701922 / $1
VOL. 137 – IRISH TUNES	00701966 / $1
VOL. 138 – BLUEGRASS CLASSICS	00701967 / $1
VOL. 139 – GARY MOORE	00702370 / $1
VOL. 140 – MORE STEVIE RAY VAUGHAN	00702396 / $1
VOL. 141 – ACOUSTIC HITS	00702401 / $1
VOL. 142 – KINGS OF LEON	00702418 / $1
VOL. 144 – DJANGO REINHARDT	00702531 / $1
VOL. 145 – DEF LEPPARD	00702532 / $1
VOL. 147 – SIMON & GARFUNKEL	14041591 / $1
VOL. 148 – BOB DYLAN	14041592 / $1
VOL. 149 – AC/DC HITS	14041593 / $1
VOL. 150 – ZAKK WYLDE	02501717 / $1
VOL. 153 – RED HOT CHILI PEPPERS	00702990 / $1
VOL. 156 – SLAYER	00703770 / $1
VOL. 157 – FLEETWOOD MAC	00101382 / $1
VOL. 158 – ULTIMATE CHRISTMAS	00101889 / $1
VOL. 160 – T-BONE WALKER	00102641 / $1
VOL. 161 – THE EAGLES – ACOUSTIC	00102659 / $1
VOL. 162 – THE EAGLES HITS	00102667 / $1
VOL. 163 – PANTERA	00103036 / $1
VOL. 166 – MODERN BLUES	00700764 / $1
VOL. 168 – KISS	00113421 / $1
VOL. 169 – TAYLOR SWIFT	00115982 / $1
VOL. 170 – THREE DAYS GRACE	00117337 / $1
VOL. 172 – THE DOOBIE BROTHERS	00119670 / $1
VOL. 174 – SCORPIONS	00122119 / $1
VOL. 176 – BLUES BREAKERS WITH JOHN MAYALL & ERIC CLAPTON	00122132 / $1
VOL. 177 – ALBERT KING	00123271 / $1
VOL. 178 – JASON MRAZ	00124165 / $1

Complete song lists available online.

Prices, contents, and availability subject to change without notice.

HAL•LEONARD CORPORATION

7777 W. BLUEMOUND RD. P.O. BOX 13819 MILWAUKEE, WI 53213

www.halleonard.com

1